HEAVEN'S HALL OF HEROES

HEAVEN'S HALL OF HEROES

FRED M. BARLOW

Illustrations by
DOUG CHAFFEE

REGULAR BAPTIST PRESS
1300 North Meacham Road
Post Office Box 95500
Schaumburg, Illinois 60195

Grateful acknowledgment is made for the kind permission of *The Biblical Evangelist,* Brownsburg, Indiana, Dr. R. L. Sumner, editor, to publish these biographical sketches in this book. These sketches first appeared as "Profiles in Evangelism," a monthly column in *The Biblical Evangelist.*

Grateful acknowledgment for permission to use quotations from other publishers is also made. Specific authors quoted will be cited in the footnotes.

Library of Congress Cataloging in Publication Data

Barlow, Fred, 1921-
    Heaven's hall of heroes.

    1. Bible—Biography. I.   Title.
BS571.B347   220.9'2   78-16887
ISBN 0-87227-062-9

DEDICATION

It is altogether appropriate that in this 25th anniversary year of the ministry of Regular Baptist Press a publication should be dedicated to RBP personnel.

Commenced in 1952 with a skeletal staff and a partial curriculum, RBP began publishing Sunday school materials in a small building in Hayward, California. A quarter century later, housed in a million dollar facility in Schaumburg, Illinois, and employing almost forty personnel, RBP publishes a total Sunday school curriculum, Christian books, plus related literature and enjoys a worldwide ministry of blessing to churches, Christian colleges, missionaries and families.

It would be impossible to list each of the workers at RBP, but to each of you, with sincerest appreciation for your love for the Lord, labors for the Lord, and lives given to the Lord, as well as for your prayerful concern and contributions to my ministry with RBP, I gratefully dedicate this volume which title truly testifies of you also: *Heaven's Hall of Heroes.*

CONTENTS

FOREWORD

This is an exciting book! Some books are written to enlighten, some to enlist, some to encourage, some to expose, some to exalt, some to enrich, and some even to entertain. *Heaven's Hall of Heroes* is all of these . . . and more.

Fred M. Barlow, one of my dearest personal friends since first meeting in our freshman seminary class well over a third of a century ago, writes as he preaches. His thrusts are aimed at the heart; his intention is to stir the emotions and change the will of his readers along lines of higher, nobler, more spiritual pursuits. That is one reason why I call this an *exciting* book.

While these biographical sketches are brief, each is amply thorough in covering the highlights of the subject's life and ministry. Dr. Barlow has an enviable and uncanny knack of getting to the heart of a personality and vividly calling attention to its outstanding characteristics, then showing how his readers may emulate those virtues in their own lives and ministries.

The author of this book serves, along with his many other activities, as a contributing editor to the monthly magazine, *The Biblical Evangelist,* and has written a regular column, "Profiles In Evangelism," almost since its inception early in 1966. It is one of the most popular features of the paper, and the sketches herein are taken from it. We are delighted that they have been compiled and released in this more permanent form, joining his previously published volume of nonbiblical personalities, *Profiles in Evangelism,* which highlights world-renowned soul-winners of past and present.

    Heaven's Hall of Heroes has our enthusiastic and unconditional commendation.

Dr. Robert L. Sumner, Director
Biblical Evangelism
Brownsburg, Indiana

PREFACE

Hebrews chapter eleven has rightly been recognized by Bible scholars through the centuries to be "God's Hall of Faith," or again, "God's Hall of Fame." Chapter twelve, continuing the sacred story, cites those heroes and heroines, calling them "a cloud of witnesses." Scripture also states of them, "Now all these things happened unto them for ensamples [pictures or types]: and they are written for our admonition . . ." (1 Cor. 10:11).

God thus penned in verbal pictures on the pages of His Scriptures biographical studies of His people to reveal the secret warnings and instruction so necessary to you and me for our daily walk, work and words.

Here is a short volume of biographical studies; sketches of those winning worthies whose lives have shone as the brightness of the sun across the centuries of human history. These are *Heaven's Hall of Heroes*—men, women, youth who wrought revivals of righteousness; who raised the standards of morality and spirituality of their day; who resisted the forces of evil; who redeemed—through their prophecies, their preaching, their pen on the pages of Holy Scriptures, their prayers—multitudes of doomed and dying sinners, bringing them to God and Christ, to a heavenly hope and Home, a transformed life and a living service.

You will meet thirty-three of these winning witnesses in this book.

Meet them in their hours of deepest conviction of sin, in their hallowed hours of conversion of soul, in their holy hours of their call to serve the Lord, and in their hallelujah hours of conquests for the Lord. Come walk with them, weep with them, work with them, win with them.

Two of these biographies belie some of the premises of the preceding paragraph. Jesus Christ is cited. Since He is the Son of God as well as the Son of man, He committed no sin, had no cause to be saved, was constrained rather than called to come "to seek and to save that which was lost." His biography as "Soul-Winner Supreme" is inserted that we may know Him better, serve Him more and love Him to the fullest! Judas Iscariot is also included in these pages, although he was never converted to Christ nor conquered for Christ. He is included here as he is shown in Scripture story: a warning to every reader to "give diligence to make your calling and election sure: for if ye do these things, ye shall never fall" (2 Pet. 1:10).

I trust these vignettes will prove vital and valuable to every reader. They are penned with a purpose: to enthuse, to encourage, to enlist a host of readers to engage all out in the worthy work of winning the lost to Christ, and then to effect a worthy walk and a winning life for Christ. Aye, "Wherefore seeing we also are compassed about with so great a cloud of witnesses, let us lay aside every weight, and the sin which doth so easily beset us, and let us run with patience the race that is set before us, Looking unto Jesus . . ." (Heb. 12:1, 2).

Fred M. Barlow

Amos

From Backwoods to Boulevard

A roll call of the elite of the evangelists of all ages reveals that many of the messengers mightily used of God were men of the fields and forests—country-reared men, rather than men trained in the centers of religious learning in the great cosmopolitan cities. Among those worthies write the name of Amos of Tekoa!

Amos must have created no small stir that day he commenced his first revival campaign (and his only recorded campaign) in Bethel. Bethel, by the way, was the Jerusalem of the kingdom of Israel, which came into being when the ten northern tribes seceded from Judah during King Rehoboam's reign. Their newly crowned king, Jeroboam, in his desire to keep the Israelites from returning to Jerusalem to worship (and thus lose their loyalties and his newly received kingdom), fashioned calves of gold and set them in Bethel, declaring this decree: "It is too much for you to go up to Jerusalem: behold thy gods, O

Israel, which brought thee up out of the land of Egypt" (1 Kings 12:28).

Jeroboam's subjects were satisfied to stay home and worship. His new religion and kingdom flourished so much that by the time of the reign of Jeroboam II, about 140 years later, Israel was a world power—prosperous and proud, but pagan and perverse.

Bethel became a seat of the temple of golden-calf worship. It was the city where the summer palace of the king "was centered with its wealth, wickedness and wantonness." Richard Day describes Bethel:

> Morality had all but perished, justice had surrendered to bribery, commerce to shoddy [dealings], and honest weights to false balances. Pilgrims coming into Bethel were waylaid and robbed by disguised priests—the very priests to whose altars the pilgrims were bound. Father and sons made a night of it and consorted with the same prostitutes![1]

Into this center of idolatry, iniquity and infamy, the rustic revivalist Amos came to preach. Shockingly enough, it was more than the herdsman's habit that commanded immediate attention of the citizenry and king of that northern kingdom. Amos was a foreigner, a prophet from the hated southern kingdom of Judah, even Jerusalem! Amazingly enough, Amos was the first prophet to come out of Judah to Israel since the "man of God" came out of Judah by the word of the Lord in the days of Jeroboam I (1 Kings 13:1). As Amos addressed himself to Israel, he adjured them of this same call, charging, "The LORD said unto me, Go, prophesy unto my people Israel" (Amos 7:15).

And Amos came preaching! Vance Havner wrote:

> He must have been a picturesque figure, strolling down Main Street, tanned and sunburned with all the marks of the countryside upon him. But if anybody in Bethel was embarrassed it was not Amos. Here was no trumpet with an uncertain sound. Here was no preacher of lavender and rosewater gospel saying, "You must repent as it were, believe in a measure, or be lost in a sense."

Amen! For Amos began his message: "The LORD will roar from Zion, and utter his voice from Jerusalem." Then he cried out: "Thus saith the LORD." I have underlined in my Bible that authority for Amos' message—"Thus saith the LORD"—fourteen times! And I underlined such statements as "saith the LORD" or the Lord GOD" twenty-eight more times. Thus over forty times Amos attested that his was a message that the Lord had spoken!

His was simple preaching. He used the imagery, the metaphors and messages that would come naturally to a shepherd, a gatherer of

14

sycamore fruit and figs in the wild wasteland country of Tekoa. But he spoke sharply, severely against sin, and surely set the style for all future evangelists, whether in the king's court or in the city churches.

Witness his words against the women at ease. "Kine of Bashan" he called them (4:1), suggesting that they were women "wandering in richest pastures, overfed, indulged, and pampered, and therefore waxed voluptuous and wanton."

Hear some other sentences of Amos—sharp, pointed, plain preaching against the sins of those pagan people:

> And I raised up of your sons for prophets, and of your young men for Nazarites. . . . But ye gave the Nazarites wine to drink; and commanded the prophets, saying, Prophesy not (2:11, 12).
> For I know your manifold transgressions and your mighty sins: they afflict the just, they take a bribe, and they turn aside the poor in the gate from their right (5:12).
> Woe to them that are at ease in Zion . . . That lie upon beds of ivory . . . That chant to the sound of the viol, and invent to themselves instruments of musick, like David; That drink wine in bowls . . . but they are not grieved for the affliction of Joseph (6:1, 4, 5, 6).

But there was a passionate plea in Amos' preaching also. Although he witnessed in warning words about the inevitable judgment—"As the shepherd taketh out of the mouth of the lion two legs, or a piece of an ear; so shall the children of Israel be taken out that dwell in Samaria" (3:12); "The Lord GOD hath sworn by his holiness, that, lo, the days shall come upon you, that he will take you away with hooks" (4:2); "I abhor the excellency of Jacob, and hate his palaces: therefore will I deliver up the city with all that is therein" (6:8); "Jeroboam shall die by the sword, and Israel shall surely be led away captive out of their own land" (7:11)—Amos pled with Israel to return unto their Redeemer: "Seek the LORD, and ye shall live" (5:6); "Prepare to meet thy God" (4:12).

It was a message Israel greatly needed, but for the most part it went unheeded. Amaziah, the high priest, called Amos' admonitions conspiracy and charged him to go home. Doubtlessly the city listened to the line and lie of the religious hireling, Amaziah, rather than to the message of revival and survival of Amos, for history records that the evangelist was expelled to his wilderness of Tekoa.

But Amos' message was not of man but from the Lord Who made him a prophet, and so history also records that the haughty house of Israel was humbled, crushed by her enemies, and carried away into servitude precisely as the prophet had proclaimed. That rejected message was penned by the prophet, the first book of prophecy to be recorded and preserved in the pages of Scripture by the Holy Spirit; and so it still proclaims to the nations today: "Therefore thus will I do unto thee . . . and because I will do this unto thee, prepare to meet thy God" (4:12).

NOTE:

1. Richard Day, *Beacon Lights of Grace* (Grand Rapids: Wm. B. Eerdmans Publishing Co., 1947), p. 23.

Daniel

The Man Who Dared

> Dare to be a Daniel,
> Dare to stand alone!
> Dare to have a purpose firm!
> Dare to make it known!

So penned the poet in one of our great Sunday school choruses. The Daniel whom he exhorted his hearers to exemplify is one of the Bible's most honored heroes.

Daniel was born in Jerusalem about 625 B.C., during the reign of King Josiah. It is certain that something of Josiah's fervent spirit, his personal piety, his reign of religious and moral reform put the steel of unbending, unflinching loyalty to his Lord God in young Daniel's soul. Jeremiah, with his faithful, fearless preaching and example, doubtlessly put more steel in Daniel's spirit. Definitely, young Daniel stood for the Lord and withstood the evil of his day, and seventy years later he was still of the same convictions and constancy!

W. A. Criswell commented:

> As the kingdom of Judah reeled dizzily in wanton idolatry and wickedness, Daniel girded himself to withstand rather than to drift with the current of his time. The great revival [under Josiah] may have been lost upon the wicked Jehoahaz and Jehoiakim and Zedekiah and Jehoiachin, but the revival found a glorious response in the hearts of Daniel and Hananiah and Mishael and Azariah.[1]

Still in his teens, Daniel, born of royal blood, possibly of the family of Hezekiah, suddenly found himself deported to Babylon. Behind him he left his beloved city of Jerusalem, burned and in rubble and ruin. He would never see it again. He was to be an exile in an alien land all his life.

Although Daniel was a captive in Babylon, he never was *of* it. Skillful in wisdom, endued with knowledge, understanding science, well favored and without blemish, soon Daniel was selected by his captors for training in the philosophies of Babylon. In that day Babylon was the seat of the most disgusting idolatries and iniquities of possibly any generation of human history. The sciences and religion were administered by stargazers, soothsayers and sorcerers who studied the heavens, dreams, visions and incantations to know the will and whims of their gods.

Daniel was subjected to such studies and every intention of the idolatrous masters to make a heathen of him. Enrolled in their school, he was expected to eat and drink their foods and wines, and his name was officially changed to honor their god Bel. Daniel, though subject to his masters, was never subjugated by their brainwashing tactics nor subverted by them. One of the thrilling tales of Old Testament story is teenage Daniel's determination not to defile himself with the king's fare—a decision that God honored and thus elevated him to a place of preeminence in the king's court.

Position and rank did not deter Daniel from continuing in fidelity to his God, even if it demanded a fearless denunciation of King Nebuchadnezzar's sins—sins that inevitably brought the king into a state of insanity. Nor did Daniel defer to Nebuchadnezzar's grandson that night in Belshazzar's banqueting hall when an awesome, armless hand wrote in unknown script upon the banquet room walls. Hastened by the trembling monarch who had previously regaled thousands of his lords and ladies in an idolatrous, blasphemous orgy, Daniel interpreted the message, rebuked his sovereign for his illicit sins and pronounced the king's and kingdom's doom. Even as Daniel declared

18

his decree, Persian armies which had secretly diverted the Euphrates River, marched up its dry beds under the ponderous, impregnable walls of Babylon—history's most fortified city. Without opposition, Cyrus' army conquered the soulless city, killed Belshazzar and commenced a reign that would dominate world history.

Again God honored Daniel, who would dare honor Him before a heathen potentate and people, and he was promoted to the first position of three presidents in the Persian kingdom. In this position, he would again show his fidelity to his faithful God in surely the severest trial of his life—a conspiracy against him by the two associate members who set out to destroy Daniel, who was then a seventy-year-old statesman.

Reasons for that conspiracy abound aplenty! Daniel's wisdom acquired through his seventy years of waiting upon his God, his purity of life achieved through seventy years of walking with his God, and his integrity to the throne through over fifty years of unimpeachable conduct were a constant rebuke to the two associate presidents: small, self-seeking men; men of corrupt policies and purposes of life; men whose sole concern was for more power and position that they may pirate more public funds! Daniel must be destroyed!

The only charge those men could level against Daniel, whose every deed, every word, every decision of his nearly seven decades had been under public scrutiny, was: "We shall not find any occasion against this Daniel, except we find it against him concerning the law of his God" (Dan. 6:5).

Then in fawning, flattering words to the king, they hypocritically engineered a decree designed to destroy Daniel. The duped and self-deceived king signed their suggestion into law: that for thirty days no man should offer prayer or petition to any god, but to the king alone.

Though Daniel knew the decree was signed and could not have been ignorant of its devices and his impending death, Daniel dared to pray publicly, keeping his windows open toward Jerusalem and praying three times daily as his manner had been in his obedience to God's command and promise in 2 Chronicles 7:12-16. John Walvoord well wrote, "Why could not he pray in secret and thus avoid breaking the king's decree? To Daniel apparently this was subterfuge, and he did not swerve whatever from his usual customs in prayer."[2]

Daniel, of course, was discovered, arraigned before the king and sentenced to be flung into a den of lions. Some of Scriptures most poignant paragraphs picture the concerned king spending a sleepless night, anxiously waiting to learn the fate of his beloved prime

19

minister. And some of Scriptures most hallelujah lines herald the triumphant greeting of the unscarred, untouched Daniel (6:14-23).

Again, God had demonstrated His great might that He might show His sovereign person and power, but also to confirm the integrity of the person and importunity of the prayer life of his beloved Daniel!

Prayer was a paramount pattern and purpose in Daniel's life. When just a youth, a conquered slave in a heathen country, Daniel and his three compatriots turned to prayer to get the needed wisdom from God to discover King Nebuchadnezzar's forgotten dream and to reveal its message (Dan. 2:17, 18). Already cited is Daniel's dedication to personal prayer, a prayer life in obedience to God's command not only in posture, but place and frequency—even when those periods of prayer meant personal death!

But the preeminence of prayer and the passionate prayer life of Daniel is best seen in chapter 9 of his book. There the elderly exile, an octogenarian who had been deported from his beloved Jerusalem as a teenage boy, understanding that the seventy-year exile of Judah prophesied by Jeremiah was terminating, set his face unto the Lord God. By prayer and supplication with fasting, sackcloth and ashes, Daniel confessed personal and national sins. Few prayers in the Bible have a peer when tried in the crucible of Daniel's concern for God's holiness; the coldness of his own heart; his concern for his beloved Jerusalem and Judah wasting, rotting in ruins; his contrition over his and his people's sins; his compassion, compulsion and consecration. Aye, Daniel prostrated in prayer, penitent, petitioning and prevailing with God. Small wonder he who was on such praying ground with God had no fears of lords and kings upon a throne, lions in a den or co-workers in a conspiracy!

As a man, Daniel possessed great spiritual characteristics. He is noted for his fidelity, loyalty, humility (5:17); godliness (6:5); devotion (6:10, 20); wisdom (1:4); importunity in his prayers; purity (1:8). Thrice he was cited by the angel of the Lord as a "dearly beloved man."

As a prophet, he was recognized by Christ (Matt. 24:15); mentioned by Ezekiel three times in his prophecy (Ezek. 14:14, 20; 28:3); and referred to in the Book of Hebrews as a man of faith (11:33).

His writings were apocalyptic, and as many scholars suggest, Daniel was the apocalypse of the Old Testament, comparing and corroborating with John's Revelation in the New Testament in hosts of areas. Every chapter of his book is actually prophetic; even the first six historical chapters picture prophetic events. But Daniel's most preeminent prophecies must be his sublime sweep of human history of the Gentile age until the advent of Christ (Dan. 2:31-45); his co-vision with Jeremiah of the seventy years of Jewish bondage (9:2); and in conjunction with this prophecy the birth and death year of Israel's Messiah (9:24-27). Thus John Walvoord wisely wrote:

> In the light of world conditions today, which would seem to anticipate the fulfillment of Daniel's time of the end, it is possible to understand Daniel today as never before in history. The hour may not be far distant when faithful saints in the midst of trial in the great tribulation will turn to these pages of Scripture and find in them the strength and courage to remain true even though it mean a martyr's death.
>
> For Christians living in the age of grace . . . the book of Daniel, as never before, casts a broad light upon contemporary events foreshadowing the consummation which may not be far distant.[3]

Daniel—the man who dared believe his God, dared obey His Word, that beloved man of God—became one of God's worthy witnesses to Christians (young and old) in these latter days—dark, desperate days, when iniquity abounds, when a fervent earnest witness for God abates, when apostasy advances!

> Dare to be a Daniel,
> Dare to stand alone!
> Dare to have a purpose firm!
> Dare to make it known!

NOTES:

1. W. A. Criswell, *Expository Sermons on the Book of Daniel,* 4 vols. (Grand Rapids: Zondervan Publishing House, 1968), I:110, 111.
2. John Walvoord, *Daniel: The Key to Prophetic Revelation* (Chicago: Moody Press, 1971), p. 138.
3. Ibid., pp. 296, 297.

David

About the King's Business

How do you describe King David? In one mind, one body, one spirit, one lifetime, no other human being could measure up to the man David, save it be that peerless personage of the New Testament—the apostle Paul!

A survey of his lifetime sounds like the resumé of a host of individuals. He was a shepherd in the field and a sovereign on the throne. He was a soldier in the battlefield, and he was a commander of battalions. He was a muse whose poetry has endured through the ages, and he was a musician whose melodies enraptured his audiences. He was an outlaw hunted as a partridge in the mountains, and he was a champion of outcasts who came to him. He was a psalmist, and he was a prophet. He was a multifold manner of man!

> David was both woefully human and wonderfully holy, daringly courageous and degradingly carnal, both magnificently regal and mundanely rueful. His great victories gained for him the heights while his vices plunged him into the depths. He was a complex man, yet a simple man. He was a man among men but also a man after God's heart. He was cognizant of the bloodshed of warfare but conversant with the blessing of worship.[1]

David was the son of Jesse, a somewhat successful sheepherder. It is evident from Scripture story that David's natural gifts and graces were not recognized by his family. The youngest son, he was given the menial task of the shepherd boy, which responsibility became preparatory school to him in its isolations and loneliness. The hardships, the privations, the challenges of his shepherd life developed in David "toughness of fibre," "power of endurance," "courage of heart," "patience to wait,"—all of which would stand him in great stead as the soldier, statesman and sovereign that he would become.

It was in those early hours of his youth that he was anointed by Samuel the seer to succeed the rejected of God King Saul. Samuel and Jesse both assumed that successor would be one of Jesse's older sons: Eliab, Abinadab, Shammah. But God, Who looks on the heart and not the outward appearance, directed Samuel to the obscurest son, David. The standards of God's selection were not rank, age, stature, personality, but the state of the heart and soul toward God. David, above all else in Israel, had that first prerequisite of leadership for the Lord. He also possessed the second requisite: the discipline of training and preparation. Aye, those sheepcote years were training ground for throne-room years. The third requirement was an absolute dependence upon the Holy Spirit of God, which attribute David exercised so often, perhaps never so evidently as when he was the young warrior alone on the battlefield against Goliath!

David as the *soldier* had no professional training for his military ministry. That military life commenced when he was but a youth, visiting the battlefield at Elah. For forty days the Israelites had been humiliated by the Philistine army and their champion, a giant called Goliath, one who measured nine and one-half feet in height. Daily Goliath challenged a Jewish soldier to fight him, winner take all! Daily he mocked their cowardice and assailed their Jehovah in cursings and blasphemies. David dared to face that foreboding foe in the name of the Lord of hosts! The rest is thrilling, God-glorifying history. His slung stone found the forehead of the leering, sneering giant, and he pitched forward—slain! David hewed off the head of that fallen champion with the giant's own sword. The Philistines fled in fear and were routed by the encouraged, ennobled Israelites. David was a hero. He would serve his nation as their supremest soldier the rest of his life, never to return again to his boyhood home as a shepherd.

For a season David commanded a crowd of outcast, ragtag, malcontents in which time he sought to defend his life against the avenging King Saul. As Israel's young sovereign he would wage a civil war in Israel until he could unite the twelve tribes into a nation under God. As their sovereign and soldier, David waged war against all surrounding nations, conquering each, one by one: Philistia, Ammon, Syria, Edom, Moab, among others. By the time of his death, David reigned over an empire that had extended its boundaries twentyfold over the territories he had inherited as successor to Saul. He was known as the "man of war," which role rendered him ineligible to fulfill the desire dearest his heart—to build the temple of God.

David gave God all the glory for his successes, stating: "Blessed be the LORD my strength, which teacheth my hands to war, and my fingers to fight. . . . He . . . subdueth my people under me" (Ps. 144:1, 2); "For by thee I have run through a troop; and by my God have I leaped over a wall" (Ps. 18:29).

At the age of thirty, David was established king of Judah upon the death of Saul. Thus began his forty-year reign as *sovereign*. His task was momentous. First, his nation had to be united. Since the days of the judges, Israel had been fragmented; every man did that which seemed to him to be right. David also had to establish a capital for his country. He began his reign in Hebron, but his spiritual sense and sensitivity to God's Spirit saw in Jerusalem (then under control of the Jebusites) the logical capital. He conquered it and converted it to become the center of his emerging nation.

> It was a masterpiece of policy and statesmanship. The capital had to be accessible to the whole nation. It also had to be strongly fortified. It had to possess great strength and beauty, to mount national pride and devotion. It must be hallowed by sacred relationships so as to be the religious center of a nation's holiest life. All these features blended in Jerusalem.[2]

The kingdom also had to be organized. Departments of law, justice, finance, military, education had to be brought into being. Priests must be mustered into service to meet the spiritual needs of the nation. In recognizing David only to be the psalmist, soldier, sweet singer of Israel, it is so easy to fail to see one of his greatest contributions to his kingdom: his organizing his nation from a volunteer, minuteman people who rallied to meet a crisis into a totally organized nation, politically, militarily, religiously. At David's death Israel was that total nation. He had been king of every one of the twelve tribes. He had given them a capital, a throne, a government and a seat of religious worship in that capital. At his death all of Israel's enemies had been subjugated. At his death there was an appointed, anointed successor in his son Solomon. David left Israel a great monarchy and left his son a great legacy.

Multifaceted man was David. He was the *sweet singer* and *psalmist* of Israel. A plentitude of psalms in the sacred Scriptures were penned by David. Some of the most majestic, most lilting, most sublime, most precious, warmest, sweetest and holiest of the 150 psalms in the sacred story were first sung by the shepherd-king. Some show his shepherd's heart (Ps. 23). Some are whispers that lay bare a lover's soul to his God (Ps. 40). Some are words wrested from a weary heart in the hours of danger or death (Ps. 142). Some are paeans of praise, happy hallelujahs rising from heart and harp (Pss. 18, 27, 33). Some are dirges, discords of a defeated, disobedient man in hours of disbelief to his God (Ps. 39). Some are prophetic portraits of the Messiah: sometimes the suffering Messiah (Ps. 22); sometimes the resurrected, reigning, righteous Ruler over the world (Pss. 16, 24, 60). Some are prayers, petitions, the pantings of a thirsty, needy soul seeking help from its God (Ps. 13). Some are psalms of sighs, sorrows over sin, the soul seeking forgiveness, cleansing, peace. Psalm 51 is the supremest psalm of this strain.

Which psalm prompts me to pen: David was a *sinner man* but also a *saintly soul*. Second Samuel 11 has to be the lowest level of David's lifetime. Those twenty-seven verses disclose David in his most dastardly deeds: adultery with Bathsheba, then the murder of her husband, Uriah, to cover up his heinous sin. Biblical record recites others of David's derelictions: his sin of ignorance or disobedience in his unscriptural decree to return the ark of the covenant to Jerusalem (2 Sam. 6); his failures to his family, both as husband and father; his sin of multiplying wives in violation of God's law (Deut. 17:17); his defiant disobedience to God's will in demanding a census (2 Sam. 24). But David's brazen immorality against Bathsheba and his cold, calculating, unconscionable murder of Uriah displeased the Lord the utmost of all David's delinquencies (2 Sam. 12).

David the sinner could and did sin to the depths of depravity, but saint that he was, he could and did repent just as deeply! Psalm 51 is the record of that repentance. Psalm 32 is the psalm of that restoration. For a long season David concealed his crimes. And in that season David lost his fellowship with his God, the song in his soul, his love for the lost, the blessed presence, peace and power of the Lord on his life. But David's confession regained it all! His confession was no perfunctory, professional, palaver of prayer. It was the broken, bleeding heart crying out to God in genuine repentance. Yea, Psalm 32 is the joy instilled, hope restored, sin forgiven, right-with-God words of a man after he had heard from Heaven.

But David, the cleansed, restored penitent, bore the chastisement of God the rest of his life because of those sins (Heb. 12:6-8). The babe born of that illicit romance died. His son Amnon committed incest against his sister Tamar under David's roof. Another son, Absalom, murdered Amnon because of that crime. Absalom then rebelled against David with Ahithophel (Bathsheba's grandfather) and stole David's throne, finally to be slaughtered in the civil war! David was smitten with some loathsome, dread disease (Pss. 38; 41:8). It was as Nathan the prophet had pronounced to David: "Now therefore the sword shall never depart from thine house; . . . Thus saith the LORD, Behold, I will raise up evil against thee out of thine own house . . . " (2 Sam. 12:10, 11).

God's grace was sufficient to David, aye, supremely sufficient. That amazing grace is shown in its most consummate capacity in this final, fullest, yet still unfulfilled promise of God to David! He would be *sire* of a greater Son, Jesus Christ, Who will rule one day on David's throne over the entire earth (2 Sam. 7:16).

David paralleled his greater Son in so many particulars: "In their anointing; their inimitable words; their sufferings; their zeal for the house of the Lord; their love for friends; their betrayal by those they had trusted; their wars; their love for Jerusalem—how much in common." But as Dr. F. B. Meyer further mused: "There the parallel stays. In His atoning death, in His incorruptible nature, in His glorious ascension the Son of David stands alone. David himself, in the Spirit, called Him Lord, and knew that He alone could fulfill the ideal kingship which no mere mortal man would ever be able to realize."[3]

NOTES:

1. Paul N. Tassell, *The Glory Years* (Schaumburg, IL: Regular Baptist Press, 1977), pp. 1, 2.

2. F. B. Meyer, *David* (Grand Rapids: Zondervan Publishing House, 1953), p. 127.

3. Ibid., p. 160.

Elijah

The Prophet of Prayer

Sometimes we say of some spiritual worthy, "He is one of a kind! When God made him, He broke the mold!" That would not be true of Elijah, for of this Tishbite (born in the mountains of Gilead in the village of Thisbe), it is said: "A man mighty in deed and word . . . and who was so eminently distinguished by Divine grace, that, when the Lord of glory Himself appeared on earth, the Jews said, 'It is Elias!' "[1] And F. W. Krummacher, who wrote that comment, could have added that the Jews mistook John the Baptist for that same Old Testament prophet. Aye, there were striking similarities in the lives of those giants sent from God!

Elijah is first introduced in 1 Kings 17:1, standing before King Ahab, of whom the Scripture shamefully states, "And Ahab did more

27

to provoke the LORD God of Israel to anger than all the kings of Israel that were before him" (1 Kings 16:33). Under Ahab's reign the land swarmed with priests of Baal and their groves. Shrines and temples to false deities of Baal and Ashtoreth saturated the scene. The altars of the Lord Jehovah were broken down and His prophets were sought out, slain with the sword. Those who named His name (about seven thousand) had gone underground in an ignoble attempt to save their lives.

It was in this hour of deepest and direst spiritual poverty and apostasy that Elijah—hated, hunted and hounded by the king —stood before Ahab and prophetically pronounced, "There shall not be dew nor rain these years, but according to my word."

This first confrontation and challenge to the king was doubtless the culmination of many, many months of prayer by the prophet. Pained in his sensitive soul over the idolatries, the sodomies, the obscenities, the apostasy of his day, and "jealous for the LORD God of hosts," Elijah had prostrated himself in prolonged periods of importunate, pleading prayer for revival and righteousness to possess the land again, and for the removal of the reproach from the holy head of his Jehovah!

As F. B. Meyer wonderfully wrote: "And in his prayer he seems to have been led back to a denunciation made, years before, by Moses to the people—that if they turned aside, and served other gods and worshipped them, the Lord's wrath would be kindled against them; and He would shut up the heavens that there should be no rain (Deut. 11:17)."[2]

The Scriptures state, "He prayed earnestly that it might not rain" (James 5:17). Any student of Scripture knows the rest of the statement: "And it rained not on the earth by the space of three years and six months." Not a drop of dew distilled upon the ground. Devastation, disease, disaster and death stalked the land. Rills and rivers were dry. Dust from the chapped and barren ground—along with the stench of the dying—swirled and stung the nostrils of the living. There was no blossom on the fig tree, nor fruit upon the vines; and the labour of the olive failed (from Hab. 3:17).

It was then that God ordered his prophet to appear the second time before the still unrepentant king: "Go, shew thyself unto Ahab; and I will send rain upon the earth" (1 Kings 18:1). That second confrontation resulted in the contest at Mount Carmel. There the 450 prophets of Baal were challenged by the prophet of Jehovah to produce fire upon their altar. Then Elijah would call upon his God to send fire upon the repaired altar of Jehovah. The consummation: "The God that answereth by fire, let him be God."

Scarcity of space prohibits more than mere mention of that contest at Carmel. "No contest" would be a more accurate conclusion. Professed prophets of the sun, the prophets of Baal, could produce no flame upon their altar, for the Word witnesses of their pleas, "There was neither voice, nor any to answer, nor any that regarded" (1 Kings 18:29). Their altar stood cold and smokeless, their bullock unconsumed.

The Bible details many beautiful and blessed prayers on its pages, but few match the majesty and might of Elijah's petition to Heaven over that repaired altar to Jehovah and its water-soaked sacrifice:

> LORD God of Abraham, Isaac, and of Israel, let it be known this day that thou art God in Israel, and that I am thy servant, and that I have done all these things at thy word. Hear me, O LORD, hear me, that this people may know that thou art the LORD God, and that thou hast turned their heart back again (1 Kings 18:36, 37).

And the Scriptures thrillingly tell:

> Then the fire of the LORD fell, and consumed the burnt sacrifice, and the wood, and the stones, and the dust, and licked up the water that was in the trench. And when all the people saw it, they fell on their faces: and they said, The LORD, he is the God; the LORD, he is the God. And Elijah said unto them, Take the prophets of Baal; let not one of them escape. And they took them: and Elijah brought them down to the brook Kishon, and slew them there (1 Kings 18:38-40).

Hours after that triumph the prophet prostrated himself again in prayer—the prayer that turned on the faucet of the skies after forty-two months of drought. God had honored His prophet's bold assertion to Ahab, "There shall not be dew nor rain these years but according to my word."

Then his unfailing, unflinching faith failed, and Elijah, hearing of the threat upon his life by the humiliated and infuriated queen, fled to the far reaches of Sinai to save his life. He was never again a factor nor a force for revival—revival that he once almost single-handedly had fired into a flame of righteousness.

Elijah taught prophets in the first school of this kind; he was translated to Heaven in a whirlwind; he appeared with Christ at the Mount of Transfiguration. But the man whom the apostle James called "the man subject to like passions" with us is best and rightly remembered as the symbol of John the Baptist, who should "go before [Jesus'] face in the spirit and power of Elijah," and the man whom the Jews first recognized in the Redeemer, as they asked of Christ, "Art thou Elias?"

NOTES:

1. F. W. Krummacher, *Elijah the Tishbite* (Grand Rapids: Zondervan Publishing House, n.d.), p. 2.
2. F. B. Meyer, *Elijah* (Grand Rapids: Zondervan Publishing House, 1954), p. 14.

Elisha

Man of God

Meet God's man for the hour in one of Israel's deepest declensions into idolatry, impurity and iniquity. I introduce you to Elisha—the man of God! Twenty-six times in 1 and 2 Kings Elisha is assigned that transcendent title! Moses wore the name. So did Elijah. And so did others of the aristocracy of Heaven. But Elisha wore that mantle of magnificence the most!

It would take a man of God to be true to God in those turbulent times during the reign of King Ahab and his vengeful and vicious Queen Jezebel, as well as in the following reigns of Jehoram and Joash. They were days of lawlessness and licentiousness. The vile worship and influences of Baal and Ashtoreth had polluted the whole national life. Idolatry had taken a hellish hold on the people for so long that the name of the true and living God had been forgotten and His temple forsaken.

Aye, to bring that nation back to its God would take a *man* of God who would believe God's promises to His people in an hour of utter unbelief, and it would take a *prophet* of God who would display God's power, mercy and forgiveness to a godless people who neither feared Him nor regarded Him. Elisha became that man!

Elisha's entrance into the prophetic ministry was as a youth when he was anointed by Elijah to be his successor. A plowboy, plowing on his father's farm, Elisha was summoned to forsake his family and follow Elijah. It was a stern test. He must give up the privileges of a doubtlessly wealthy home to endure the privations and persecutions that would be his immediately upon his identification and ministration with Elijah, hated and hounded by Queen Jezebel and her retinue of priests—and, of course, the vilification he would ever endure the rest of his life as a prophet of Jehovah God in an apostatized nation.

Elisha chose to follow Elijah. "He . . . took a yoke of oxen, and slew them, and boiled their flesh with the instruments of the oxen, and gave unto the people, and they did eat" (1 Kings 19:21). That feast meant a finality to family, friends and fortune in order to follow God, a burning of all bridges behind him, for "then he arose, and went after Elijah, and ministered unto him" (1 Kings 19:21).

Probably ten years Elisha was being prepared to become the successor of Elijah. Successor is not meant to suggest that Elisha would be an imitator, a rubber stamp copy of his senior prophet. Elijah's ministry was stormy, severe, sharp, a constant rebuke to King Ahab and his court. His pronouncements were doom-heralding, death-dealing, sin-rebuking, repentance-demanding. The heavens denied water for three years to a burnt, chapped, barren, wasteland earth at Elijah's demand to Deity. Altar-cleansing, sacrifice-consuming fire fell at that prophet's petition to demonstrate God's judicial power, His maligned majesty and His holy anger with a nation that had forsaken Him to follow idols.

Elisha's ministry was of a milder manner. His primary purpose, albeit the same as Elijah's—to emphasize God's holiness, majesty and power rejected and ridiculed by Israel—was also to demonstrate divine mercy, forbearance and forgiveness to any and all who would return to their rejected Redeemer.

Fourteen miracles, plus a long life—faith-filled, Spirit-of-God submitted, daily dedicated to glorify God before kings or commoners, Jews or Gentiles, saints or sinners—were the mighty marks that Elisha, the man of God, left upon Israel.

Recount some of those mighty miracles under that man of God; miracles that magnified God in many cities and nations—Samaria,

32

Syria, Shunem, Moab; miracles that glorified God before kings, generals, captains, prophets, widows, servants; miracles that championed God's cause in winning wars, raising the dead, healing the sick, helping the poor, calling a people back to its God.

You read right when you read fourteen miracles. That tremendous total doubtless had its origin back that day when Elijah was translated into the heavens. After crossing the Jordan River dry-shod, because of Elijah's miracle of smiting and splitting the waters asunder, Elijah asked Elisha, "Ask what I shall do for thee, before I be taken away from thee. And Elisha said, I pray thee, let a double portion of thy spirit be upon me." (2 Kings 2:9).

That request meant many things. Surely, first and foremost, it was a petition for the birthright of a firstborn from his father (Deut. 21:17)—in this case, a spiritual relationship and a spiritual request. That Elisha's request was granted is evidenced in fourteen recorded miracles—exactly twice the seven recorded of Elijah.

The first miracle of Elisha, and probably the most vital to his ministry and testimony, was that he, too, smote the waters of the Jordan with the mantle of the ascended Elijah, in the name of the Lord God of Elijah, and "they parted hither and thither: and Elisha went over." That miracle made full proof of his ministry, and Elisha became the worthy successor of Elijah. He would heal the death-dealing waters of Jericho; raise the widow's son from the dead; multiply a widow's cruse of oil; heal Syria's famed leprous captain, Naaman. But, assuredly, the most amazing of his miracles, the fourteenth, occurred after his death. God honored Elijah by taking him from this earth without death, but Elisha died a natural death after a long, full life. Buried in a cave excavated out of a rock, Elisha's body had decomposed until only his bones remained. One day some Jews were preparing to bury a corpse nearby when they were startled by a band of marauding Moabites. Before fleeing to find a place of safety, they cast the corpse into Elisha's sepulchre, and the Scriptures state: "And when the man was let down, and touched the bones of Elisha, he revived, and stood up on his feet" (2 Kings 13:21). As Arthur Pink penned:

> It was the Lord's seal upon His servant's mission. It was an intimation that other miracles would yet be wrought for Israel in response to his prayers and as a result of his labors. Thus to the end, miracles are connected with the mission of Elisha.[1]

But Elisha's ministry meant more than miracles. He had instructed the people and the sons of the prophets (the latter in what is recognized as schools) in the *work,* the *Word* and the *will* of God. He had interceded in prayer before God for the kings and the country. He had been the man of God intervening between Israel and her enemies in great emergencies. He had been the defense, the arm of deliverance for more than one king of Israel. So confirmed the young King Joash as he came to the bedside of the dying prophet and sobbed out, "O my father, my father, the chariot of Israel, and the horsemen thereof" (2 Kings 13:14). It was an eloquent testimonial that Elisha was truly a man of God!

Need it be added that such is the one and only hope for our Christless, corrupted and collapsing nation!

NOTE:

1. Arthur W. Pink, *Gleanings from Elisha* (Chicago: Moody Press, 1972), p. 254.

Esther

Courage Born of Compassion

Queen Esther is one of my favorite heroines of sacred story. Great and noble women are listed in God's ledger who left a legacy of righteousness, revival and reformation to a wicked and weary world. Queen Esther is surely one of the foremost of that female company.

Her story reads like a stranger-than-fiction thriller, a Ripley's "Believe It or Not" experience. But her life was another of those true, thrilling histories of the sovereign God of Heaven working in mysterious ways His wonders to perform. In a single sentence, Esther's story is the chronicle of a Jewish slave in a heathen land who risked her life and saved her race from inevitable extinction.

Judah had been carried into captivity in 586 B.C. by the Babylonians, who in turn capitulated to the Persians. The story of

Esther transpired about 100 years after the captivity of Judah when Persia ruled the then known world—an empire that stretched over 1500 miles and embraced 127 provinces from India to Ethiopia. Authorities agree that the events in her life occurred between the sixth and seventh chapters of the Book of Ezra, a time when both secular and sacred history record the reign of Xerxes, or Ahasuerus, in the capital city of Shushan.

The king's court was corrupt, one evidence being a bizzare ball that lasted 180 days (half a year) in which the king, his courtiers and his countrymen became intoxicated, jaded, stupored. It was at such a feast, the reveling, bacchanalian, debauched monarch commanded his queen, Vashti, to parade immodestly before his drunken, dissipated lords and ladies. Vashti, "a rare gem in the midst of that corruption, valorous, womanly, refusing to sacrifice her honor, dignity, self respect" rejected the royal summons. In so doing, Xerxes, slave to his depraved passions and despotic in his powers, banished his queen.

Here Esther enters the scene. Orphaned of her parents and raised by an elder cousin, Mordecai, this Jewess was selected to be an entrant in an empire-wide beauty contest, the winner to be crowned queen in Vashti's stead. It is evident that Esther possessed an outward beauty, and an inward one as well, because she was quickly pushed to the forefront by the king's chamberlain. She was chosen by the king to become his new bride and queen. Upon counsel from her cousin, Esther never revealed her race, and thus Scripture records Esther engaged in direct disobedience to the Lord's commands to Israel which forbade the daughters of Israel being given in marriage to the Gentiles. Esther's and Mordecai's deed has been the source of much controversy and question among scholars of Scripture, occasioning one to remark, "Providence had placed him [Moses] in Pharaoh's house, but faith took him out of it. With Esther it was otherwise."[1]

Why Mordecai and Esther concealed their religion and race and why Esther entered into an unholy alliance in marriage with the Gentile monarch are subject to speculation. The Scriptures are silent on the subject. How God would have intervened and saved His people from the destruction that was then being plotted is also speculation. Harry Ironside interpreted it well when he wrote,

> Although in an unscriptural position, God who knows the heart of His servant, who sees in Mordecai and Esther true lovers of Israel, will use them signally for His own ends of good to His people, whom He truly loved. If they cover their nationality, and shame Him so that He hides His name too, He will make them nevertheless the instruments of His providence.[2]

First, He magnified Mordecai. Seated in the king's gate, Mordecai overheard a plot by two of the king's chamberlains to assassinate Ahasuerus. Mordecai forwarded the disclosure to Esther, who forewarned the king of Mordecai's discovery. The plot was foiled, the conspirators hanged, and Mordecai's deed apparently was forgotten. However the purposes of God prevailed again. One night the king was sleepless, an insomnia doubtlessly induced by Deity. In his sleeplessness he called for the chronicles of the kingdom to be read to him. There and then he learned of Mordecai's intervention to save his life, which incident triggered Mordecai's eventual promotion to prime minister.

But not without the harassment and hatred of Haman, son of Hammedatha the Agagite, promoted in position by the king over all his princes, and reverenced by every prince and the peoples of Shushan save Mordecai. Worshiper of Jehovah alone, Mordecai refused to bow before Haman. Haman was humiliated and infuriated, his vanity piqued. To placate his pained ego he plotted to exterminate Mordecai and his race—genocide of the Jews.

That diabolical scheme was approved by the gullible king and became an unalterable law. The pronouncement was proclaimed throughout the kingdom of the day of the destruction of every Jew.

Haman, a most unworthy man, is worthy of cursory consideration. An Agagite, a nation perpetually the enemy of the Jews, Haman personified that hatred. B. H. Carroll commented of Haman: "That man's name is a synonym for vanity and fulsome pride, ruthlessness and savagery, deceit, cruelty, and all that is ignoble. He is the incarnation of insane conceit. Honors made a fool of him. . . . It was this man's vanity that led to his downfall."[3]

Esther learned of that death-dooming decree from Mordecai. He admonished her that she must intercede for her people before the king. Mordecai's charge to the queen contained two great truths: "And who knoweth whether thou art come to the kingdom for such a time as this?" (4:14), and, "Think not with thyself that thou shalt escape in the king's house, more than all the Jews" (4:13).

Esther's exposé of her race and religion to the king is one of literature's loftiest utterances. Not until she, her ladies and Mordecai fasted for three days did Esther dare to pour out her heart to her heathen husband. It was no selfish supplication to save her own life. Rather it was an entreaty born of total selflessness, a brokenhearted compassion for her own race. Out of that burdened heart and anguished soul, Esther importuned the king: "How can I endure to see the destruction of my kindred?" Her race was under the indictment of death. Haman's mad and merciless maneuvering had made a mandate of death for "all Jews, both young and old, little children and women." That awesome decree crushed her heart, consumed her mind, incited her to risk her life: "For how can I endure to see the evil that shall come unto my people? or how can I endure to see the destruction of my kindred?" (8:6).

God, Who moves kings' heads and hearts (Prov. 21:1), honored that maiden's compassionate confession. The king shockingly, shamefully discovered the enormity and iniquity of his signature on that statute. He had been duped by Haman. He had signed the death decree of an entire race. That decree was irrevocable by the law of the Medes and Persians.

But Ahasuerus acted. Again, only a summary, citing no detail of the intrigue and suspense of the actions, the king decreed the death of Haman and his household, retributively upon the gallows Haman had built for Mordecai's death. Ahasuerus mustered Mordecai to draft another decree which would save the lives of the Jews, yet still keep the letter of the prior paper. The new decree dictated: "Wherein the king granted the Jews which were in every city to gather themselves together, and to stand for their life, to destroy, to slay, and to cause to perish, all the power of the people and province that would assault them, both little ones and women, and to take the spoil of them for a prey" (8:11).

It has to be one of history's storied accomplishments—the circulation of that commission to the Jews to save their lives. It was emergency evangelism. No moment could be lost. Life and death were in the balance. Urgency was the watchword. There were 127 provinces spreading over 1500 miles and no telephones, no telegraphs, no radio, no TV, no railroads, no airplanes. Tardiness of only one minute could cost thousands of needless deaths. "So the posts that rode upon mules and camels went out, being hastened and pressed on by the king's commandment."

To the glory of God, to the praise of the postmen, to the salvation of a doomed race, the furthermost hamlet was reached in time, the Scriptures citing: "And in every province, and in every city, whithersoever the king's commandment and his decree came, the Jews had joy and gladness." Mourning turned to rejoicing!

Which pronouncement prompts me to pen—in our awful hour of forthcoming judgment from a thrice holy God—when will we Christians shake off our lethargic, anemic efforts in evangelism and, in full obedience to Christ our King, go all out, in a full-scale, intense effort to evangelize every creature with the King's gospel pardon?

38

Esther's Bible biography concludes with consummate glories: Esther and her people spared; their enemies conquered; Mordecai crowned prime minister of Persia; the Feast of Purim (lots) to celebrate those victories instituted.

Yes, the Book of Esther is a thrilling, true recital of God's sovereign purposes and power. Hundreds of highlights crisscross its every page. This study could only cite a fraction of the facts stranger than fiction. But in my estimation the highlight of the text is the evangelistic fervor of Esther, who would risk her safety, security, aye, her own life for her love for her doomed people. The evangelism that fired her soul sparked and spread into a flame that shined into 127 provinces, changing destinies for hundreds and thousands.

The same sort of a spiritual fire needs to be kindled in our dark day. May God grant it is my earnest prayer!

NOTES:

1. Harry Ironside, *Notes on the Book of Esther* (Neptune, NJ: Loizeaux Brother, Inc., 1921), p. 24.
2. Ibid., p. 31.
3. B. H. Carroll, *An Interpretation of the English Bible,* 6 vols. (Grand Rapids: Baker Book House, 1976), 2:251.

Ezra

The Scribe Evangelist

Sometimes in one sentence of Scripture the Spirit of God gives us the entire sweep of a man. So it is in Ezra 7:10. There the Lord lays His line of measurement upon a man whose ministry was to result in the great awakening of a sinful, enslaved nation of Israel. God's record reads of that evangelist: "For Ezra had prepared his heart to seek the law of the LORD, and to do it, and to teach in Israel statutes and judgments."

Readers will remember that Israel in Ezra's day was in bondage in Babylon. For seventy years they had been a stranger in a strange land. That seven-decade captivity had been the price tag to cure the Jews for denying God His Sabbaths, desecrating His laws and dethroning Him from their hearts, their homes and their help for the gods of other nations. Then, as Hyman Appelman attested, "The seventy years of

Babylonian captivity had dragged to their weary end. The Lord had put it into the hearts of the Persian conquerors of Babylon to restore the Jews to their homeland."[1]

Sad to say, most Jews were content in that land of captivity. Many were reluctant to leave it for the hardships and dangers of the return journey and the rigors of rebuilding those burned out, blackened ruins of desolation and destruction.

But Ezra was one who was ready for the return home, the restoration of the nation, the rebuilding of the torn-down temple. He was a scribe and a priest. As such, it is evident Ezra had pored over the pages of the prophecies of God, for as the Scriptures state: "Ezra had prepared his heart to seek the law of the LORD." And it is equally evident those words from Heaven had burned into his brain, quickened and controlled his conscience, excited his emotions, stirred his soul, swept away his sins, and purified and empowered his purpose and passion to serve his God!

Those high, holy behests from Heaven impelled the man to minister the same transforming truths to others, for he taught "Israel statutes and judgments." Soon a host of Hebrews had been revived and were ready to return to Jerusalem to serve their true and living God.

Ezra's expedition was no modest mission. He was entrusted with the vessels originally used in the Temple before being brought to Babylon. And he was to carry back huge sums of money and much merchandise. It was an 800-mile journey through robber-infested, alien territories. Perils could be expected anytime, all the time, any place, every place. Prudence would petition the king for an escort to protect life and property, but such a proposition embarrassed Ezra, who realized such a request before a heathen king was an insult to God's greatness and goodness, and would impugn the testimony Ezra had given of his God: "The hand of our God is upon all them for good that seek him" (Ezra 8:22). So the priest sought no help from heathen royalty, but petitioned Heaven's God, "to seek of him a right way for us, and for our little ones, and for all our substance" (8:21).

Ezra's faith was not futile or fatal, but fruitful, for he and his host arrived and Ezra exclaimed of his God, "He delivered us from the hand of the enemy, and of such as lay in wait by the way" (8:31). Aye, the troupe and their treasure arrived safe and sure. The vessels were consecrated, the wealth invested in God's treasury, the sacrifices at the altar renewed. Revival had been rekindled!

But the joys from that journey were not long lasting. God's people had come out of Babylon, but the spirit of that morally and spiritually corrupt country had not been left behind. An iniquity-infested Israel soon was intermarrying and intermingling with the uncircumcised in their homeland.

The purity and spirituality of the priest were piqued by those abominable alliances. So much so that Ezra expressed his experience, "And when I heard this thing, I rent my garment and my mantle, and plucked off the hair of my head and of my beard, and sat down astonied" (9:3).

Then that priest prayed! Ezra's entreaty to God for his people in their impurity must rank as one of the most illustrious examples of intercessory prayer recorded in Scripture. It bleeds with brokenheartedness, pulses with penitence, bares the soul crushed in confession of sin. It is the prayer of a priest looking at sin and loathing sin in the eyes of a holy, sin-hating God. It is the prayer of a priest identifying himself with the impurities of his people and entreating God for mercy, for forgiveness, for cleansing.

May that centuries-old prayer speak to our sinfulness, our shallowness, our shamelessness as we read only a portion of that petition:

> . . . Having rent my garment and my mantle, I fell upon my knees, and spread out my hands unto the LORD my God, And said, O my God, I am ashamed and blush to lift up my face to thee, my God: for our iniquities are increased over our head, and our trespass is grown up unto the heavens. . . . For we have forsaken thy commandments. . . . O LORD God of Israel, thou art righteous: for we remain yet escaped, as it is this day: behold, we are before thee in our trespasses: for we cannot stand before thee because of this (9:5, 6, 10, 15).

Ezra's prayer was efficacious, for the Scriptures state:

> Now when Ezra had prayed, and when he had confessed, weeping and casting himself down before the house of God, there assembled unto him out of Israel a very great congregation of men and women and children: for the people wept very sore. . . . and said unto Ezra, We have trespassed against our God . . . yet now there is hope in Israel concerning this thing. Now therefore let us make a covenant with our God to put away [sin] (10:1-3).

And Israel kept her promise to her priest. There was repentance, a rending of those heathen alliances, and a return to God. It took three months for all the registry of those who had transgressed the commandments to make their restitution and be restored—but the result was a revived nation under God!

In our day of similar depravity and degeneracy in an America that has deserted God, desecrated His day, defiled our land and denied God's Word, Christians often feel so helpless and hopeless to try to turn a nation back to God. May the shining example of Ezra enlighten, encourage, energize us that even one person with a prepared heart, a holy purpose to follow God's law, and a Holy Spirit of God empowering to teach His statutes and judgments, can restrain that nation from the wrong and return it to the right and to revival! And may each reader set out today to be that person!

NOTE:

1. Hyman Appelman, "Ezra Speaks to America," *Sword of the Lord* (August 11, 1972), p. 1.

Habakkuk

The Prophet of Revival

Even a casual reading of the three short chapters of this prophecy reveals to the reader the desperate earnestness of the man Habakkuk. Prophet during the days of King Josiah, Habakkuk had seen a sampling, a showering of mercy drops, of revival in the reign of that righteous king (2 Kings 22:18-20). But later on in the reign of the succeeding King Jehoiakim, Habakkuk witnessed his nation backslide into the grossest immoralities. God had been dethroned, His word and warnings denied, His commandments disregarded, His temple deserted of worshipers, His prophets debauched! Drunkenness had become rife, rampant (2:5, 15); debauchery was the role of both priests and people; deadness to morality, to spirituality, to the ethical reigned in the nation that had been *conceived* by God to be His righteous people, *commanded* by God to be a holy people, and *counted* on by God to be the mirroring jewel of Jehovah among all the nations of the world.

That apostasy, anarchy and abounding iniquity had broken the holy-hearted Habakkuk. Small wonder he sobbed out in sorrowing words the first sentence of his prophecy, "The burden which Habakkuk the prophet did see." The word *burden* prepared his people to expect a solemn utterance. Solemn it was. Unlike other prophets, Habakkuk did not essentially deliver a message of denunciation against the sins of his people or some foreign people. His speech is especially directed to God, actually a colloquy between Habakkuk and God in which he seeks solution to a most pressing problem.

Habakkuk's problem with God was twofold. First, the Chaldean nation had embarked on a ruthless campaign of conquest of the world. Nineveh and Egypt had already capitulated to the violent, villainous tyrannical conquerors. Lebanon at that hour was under severe seige. Judah was next. Habakkuk was a perplexed prophet. The depravity of his own people pained and pierced his holy heart. But the prospect of Jehovah's chosen people being conquered, then consumed by the Chaldeans, a totally godless, unrighteous nation, plagued Habakkuk's sense of spiritual values.

That prosperity of the Chaldeans occasioned his second perplexity: God's seeming inactivity to intervene and save Judah and shower His vengeance upon the Chaldeans. Thus Habakkuk cried out his complaint to God. It was almost akin to today's false and foreign God-is-dead philosophy. Simply stated, Habakkuk's concern was: how could Jehovah raise up such a rapacious, vicious nation, empower and enable it to execute judgment upon Judah, admittedly wicked, but definitely more righteous than the enemy which was destined to destroy Judah? Habakkuk could not reconcile that inequity with the God who "art of purer eyes than to behold evil, and canst not look on iniquity" (1:13).

The thrice holy God of Heaven answered Habakkuk. To the prophet's enigma, Jehovah "enunciated the great moral principle of true religion"[1]—the prosperity of the wicked, whether it be an individual or it be national, is a transitory, temporal prosperity. "Pride, tyranny cannot from the nature of them endure, but the righteous, if only stedfast, shall survive,"[2] for "the just [righteous one] shall live by his faith" (2:4).

That great text, that great truth (2:4) was Habakkuk's greatest contribution to the theology of the world—the truth of justification by faith. Paul penned that paramount precept to the churches in Rome

45

(Rom. 1:17) and Galatia (Gal. 3:11), but Habakkuk heralded it first. Augustine announced that dogma in his day, but Habakkuk had held high that truth twelve centuries before. Martin Luther rallied the reformers about this standard and led multitudes out of the shackling, enslaving sacramental and sacerdotal chains of Catholicism; but Habakkuk first raised the standard two millennia earlier when thrones were tottering, war was raging, righteousness seemed rescinded and the chosen people of God were about to perish from the earth.

It was in that horror hour, that hopeless hour, that holocaust hour, Habakkuk's faith leaped the labyrinth of that doomed day and saw the salvation and security of God's people in the faithfulness of God and in Israel's faithfulness to God. As B. H. Carroll commented on that passage, "The word here is 'faithfulness,' not merely faith. The root of it is the word which means faith and from which we get our word, 'amen.' It means faithfulness, integrity, perserverance, and especially, stedfastness."[3]

That truth today is the Balm of Gilead to ease the hurt of the sin-sick soul; the Light of Life to disperse the darkness of the sin-darkened soul; the Cleansing Stream to wash white and pure the sin-stained soul. Especially in that larger light the apostle Paul preached it in view of the atoning, sacrificial, soul-justifying salvation secured by Christ's crucifixion and resurrection.

Reconciled to the righteousness of God's government over the nations, assured of the Lord of the justifying fruit of faith and faithfulness, Habakkuk was faithful to pen the punishment that must be inflicted upon the iniquitous: the Chaldeans for certain, Judah justly, Israel indeed, all nations notwithstanding. Habakkuk wrote those woes as a song to be sung: the plunderer will be plundered in return (2:6-8); evil wrought upon another will be recompensed with evil (2:9-11); the trafficker in booze shall suffer the blighting ruin of booze (2:15-17); civilizations built upon bloodshed will be the fuel for the fires of God's judgments (2:15-17); and the idolater will become as ignorant as his idols (2:18, 19). Two and one-half millennia of history have been written since those warnings of woe were written by Habakkuk, but they are just as correct in their condemnation and consequences today.

In chapter three of his prophecy, we see the heart of Habakkuk laid bare before his God. Even his name becomes worthy of analysis, because his name—peculiar, unique to Habakkuk alone—reveals much, yea mightily, the man. The name *Habakkuk* means "to embrace, or one embraced." Ancient rabbis taught that Habakkuk was a prophet born of the Shunammite woman in the days of Elisha in the nineteenth century B.C., associating his name with Elisha's promise to that woman of giant faith, "Thou shalt embrace a son." Most likely his name was associated with his life-laying-hold-of holiness and his hold and embrace on his love for his God.

That heartbeat, that hunger for God's holiness in his life—and in the lives and upon the lips of others—is heard in his passionate prayer: "Revive thy work" (3:2). The prayer is actually a petition to God in poetry, as most of the book is sublimest poetry. As such, Habakkuk's hymn of prophecy and poetry is considered one of the Hebrews' classical books, comparable in literary excellence and genius to the prophecy of Isaiah. Habakkuk was much akin to Isaiah; he was a prophet who had seen, had been smitten down by, and who had been sensitized by the holiness of Jehovah. Jealous for God's holiness, zealous to convert his nation to the holiness of God, Habakkuk thus penned one of Israel's immortal works.

What we know about Habakkuk is not what we read about him in the other Scriptures because there is no other record of the man. What we know of him is what we see revealed in his words—three pages in my Bible. But in that vigorous and soul-stirring prophetic poem which vividly, dramatically, almost in a too intimate discourse with Deity to be revealed to others, we learn much about the man Habakkuk. Nowhere else do we learn him better than when we see him, with his heart bared before his God, bowed down, heart broken until it can break no more, bleeding until it can bleed no more, beg in bursting words and burdened soul this parmount petition: "O LORD [Yahweh], revive thy work in the midst of the years, in the midst of the years make known; in wrath remember mercy" (3:2).

Aye, when you poll the names of the prophets of God, write in large letters—HABAKKUK—the prophet of revival!

NOTES:

1. George L. Robinson, *The Twelve Minor Prophets* (Grand Rapids: Baker Book House, 1972), p. 123.
2. Ibid.
3. B. H. Carroll, *An Interpretation of the English Bible,* 6 vols. (Grand Rapids: Baker Book House, 1976), 3:22.

Hezekiah

Truehearted, Wholehearted

When God's Holy Spirit pens His appraisal of a person, you can be sure it is the faithful, full estimation of the individual. The Spirit's specification on King Hezekiah, who was also in his lifetime a soldier, statesman, architect, poet as well as a king, is stated in 2 Kings 18:5 and 6: "He trusted in the LORD God of Israel; so that after him was none like him among all the kings of Judah, nor any that were before him. For he clave to the LORD, and departed not from following him, but kept his commandments, which the LORD commanded Moses."

Twentieth-century sociologists would have decided difficulty attempting to explain Hezekiah's greatness and goodness, his moral and spiritual stability and successes in light of his environment and heredity. As to heredity, he was the son of King Ahaz, of whom the Scriptures shamefully state: "For the LORD brought Judah low because of Ahaz king of Israel; for he made Judah naked [the word is rightly rendered "cast away all restraint"], and transgressed sore against the LORD" (2 Chron. 28:19).

As to Hezekiah's environment, the moral and spiritual bankruptcy of Ahaz and his reign of ruin is distressingly described in such statements as these: "For he walked in the ways of the kings of Israel, and made also molten images for Baalim. Moreover he burnt incense in the valley of the son of Hinnom, and burnt his children in the fire. . . . He sacrificed also and burnt incense in the high places, and on the hills, and under every green tree" (2 Chron. 28:2-4). (The image erected was called Molech, an Ammonite god, and was actually a furnace in human form. Babies were laid into the arms of that image to be burned as sacrifices to that spurious god.) Ahaz also "sacrificed unto the gods of Damascus, which smote him: and he said, Because the gods of the kings of Syria help them, therefore will I sacrifice to them, that they may help me. But they were the ruin of him, and of all Israel. And Ahaz gathered together the vessels of the house of God, and cut in pieces the vessels of the house of God, and shut up the doors of the house of the LORD, and he made him altars in every corner of Jerusalem. And in every several city of Judah he made high places to burn incense unto other gods . . ." (28:23-25). Sorcery and witchcraft were accentuated in Ahaz's reign. Some scholars suggest that his temple steps were built to a platform and sundial, all designed so he could worship the signs of the zodiac. The first five chapters of Isaiah's prophecy portray in direst detail the depravity of Ahaz, his court and his people.

But out of that godless, immoral morass and spiritual vacuum, the 25-year-old Hezekiah came to the throne of Judah. He led his people into one of its greatest revivals in its spiritual history, as well as one of its periods of greatest prosperity and preeminence among the nations. "It is not often that a king is a good, praying man, for piety does not usually thrive in the pomp and luxury of a palace. Living in regal grandeur and exercising unlimited authority is not conducive to consecrated living." But Hezekiah, despite his heredity and his environment, was an exception to the rule, and as God's Spirit stated, he was one of Israel's godliest, greatest monarchs.

Immediately upon ascension to the throne Hezekiah initiated sweeping reforms. Notable was his destruction of those idolatrous high places fashioned by his father in defiance of divine decrees. Hezekiah boldly broke in pieces the brazen serpent which Moses had made in obedience to the Lord in the wilderness at Mt. Hor (Num. 21:4-9). Incredibly, "unto those [Hezekiah's] days the children of Israel did burn incense to it: and he called it Nehushtan [meaning "it is only a piece of brass"]" (2 Kings 18:4).

Incredible is the right word. Incredible it is that such veneration of a relic had been tolerated by such godly leaders in Israel as Samuel, David and Asa, among others. One can only speculate as to the fierce, frenzied reactions of those fanatical idolaters when they learned of Hezekiah's contempt for and his smashing in pieces their sacred serpent.

Then Hezekiah renovated the Temple that his father had polluted with idolatrous altars and corrupted with pagan practices. The doors of the Temple were opened again; the uncleanness carried abroad to Brook Kidron; the altar rebuilt; the blood of sacrifices spilled on it again; the furnishings restored to their proper places; the Levitical choir reinstituted. *Judah had a revival,* its first spiritual awakening and quickening since the days of King Asa, for we read, "When the burnt offering began, the song of the LORD began also" (2 Chron. 29:27). This is the first reference to God's people singing in joy to the Lord in 300 years!

Reviewing that revival, "we find words indicating sanctification and holiness, twenty-six times in seventy-two verses, a constant recurring of such words as *cleanse, consecrate, purification, holiness,* the *Holy Place, holy things,* and especially the verb, *sanctify,* which occurs fourteen times."[1]

Suffice it to say, the elements which produced Hezekiah's revival are the essentials to revival in any and every hour, especially in these tottering times: reemphasis of the proclamation and practice of God's Word, repentance and renouncing of personal sin in our lives, returning to God for mercy and cleansing, restoring the broken altars of prayer, personal separation, obedience, Bible study, soul-winning, dedication, then REVIVAL, REFRESHING, REJOICING: the song of the Lord!

Included in the revival of Hezekiah, and not incidental but imperative to it, was his call for Israel to observe the Passover. God witnesses of Hezekiah's: "For since the time of Solomon . . . there was not the like in Jerusalem. Then the priests the Levites arose and blessed the people: and their voice was heard, and their prayer came up to his holy dwelling place, even unto heaven" (2 Chron. 30:26, 27).

Hezekiah was not only a tower of strength to turn his nation back to God, he was a prince in prayer who turned a besieging army back to Assyria in defeat. Ahaz's sins had brought Judah into a tributary state to Assyria. Hezekiah, encouraged by Isaiah's prophecy against Assyria, determined to throw off that yoke. He stopped the tribute payments to King Sennacherib. (What an influence for good Isaiah had on Hezekiah!) Assyria's armies retaliated, invaded Judah and shortly had Jerusalem in a strangling siege. An ultimatum was delivered to Hezekiah: surrender or be sacked!

One of Scriptures most sacred scenes must be the hour when the beleaguered King Hezekiah took that letter before the Lord. The letter derided in insolent language Hezekiah's faith in the God of Israel and in scorning insult defied Jehovah, asserting Assyria's invincibility against any and all gods. "Hezekiah went up unto the house of the LORD, and spread it before the LORD and . . . prayed unto the LORD" (Isa. 37:14, 15) to deliver his people from an impossible situation. That precious prayer is recorded in Isaiah 37:16-20. Heaven answered! Isaiah's prophecy was fulfilled! The Assyrian army never entered the city! An angel of the Lord slaughtered 185,000 troops that night! Sennacherib and the remnant of his army retreated home! Judah was saved! God was glorified! Hezekiah's faith was vindicated! It was a great, glorious, hallelujah hour in Judah's history!

Israel was also indebted to Hezekiah for his poetical influences upon his people. His greatest contribution was to put in order the canon of Scripture extant in his day. He made a compilation of proverbs, and he restored the use of David's and Asaph's psalms in worship in the Temple. It is evident Hezekiah compiled them into books as we now know them in the Authorized Version, and scholars of the Psalms suggest that those psalms signified "songs of degrees" were initialed in the Hebrew HZK, Hezekiah. Isaiah 38 is the Holy Spirit's record of one of Hezekiah's poems. Read it and hear the heartbeat of the man.

Hezekiah was a most illustrious king. Riches and honor came to him, so much so that he has often been compared to Solomon in his wealth, his works, his fame. Which comment leads me to consider Hezekiah's two greatest qualities: his simple and sincere faith in his God and his simple and sincere prayers to his God. God was real to Hezekiah. He believed Jehovah lived and ruled, and so he believed in His promises, purposes and power. Such faith eradicated idolatry in the land, rallied his people's return to God and righteousness, and reinforced their courage in the siege by the Assyrians.

Hezekiah's prayer life was equally vital. He prayed to God and received answers from God in times of national emergency, invoking God's intervention for protection and for provision for his nation. And he prayed just as successfully in times of personal extremity, the most outstanding instance being his prayer for recovery from his death-dealing disease. God granted him fifteen years extension of life.

Sad to say, in that extended time, Hezekiah's honors precipitated pride in the once humble and holy king. That pride peaked when Hezekiah, flushed with his successes, showed an embassage from Babylon—enemy spies rather than earnest admirers—all of his treasures, armies and policies. This incident along with other acts of vanity vented the wrath of God upon the king, who, like all of us too often, failed to render to God the praise for all His mighty works.

Yet despite that declension, Hezekiah was the most commended king in the dynasty of King David until Christ reigns. Surely the real reason for the Spirit's singular praise of the man was what He saw in Hezekiah's heart. We read of the king's heart: "It is in mine *heart* to make a covenant with the LORD God of Israel" (2 Chron. 29:10). Again, "And in every work that he began in the service of the house of God, and in the law, and in the commandments, to seek his God, he did it with all his heart, and prospered" (2 Chron. 31:21). The Holy Spirit's summary of Hezekiah: he was a truehearted, wholehearted man!

NOTE:

1. Wilbur Smith, *The Glorious Revival Under King Hezekiah* (Grand Rapids: Zondervan Publishing House, 1954), p. 41.

Jeremiah

The Prince of the Prophets

The most exquisite sensibility of soul was Jeremiah's singular and
sovereign distinction above all the other Hebrew prophets. . . . Such
another child for sensibility of soul was not born of woman until the Virgin
Mary brought forth the Man of Sorrows Himself. . . . No [other] prophet
of them all stands in reality so near to Jesus Christ. Jeremiah is the true
forerunner of our Lord.[1]

Small wonder, then, that at Caesarea Philippi discerning disciples
declared that Jesus was "come back again as Jeremiah," that prophet
with the broken, bleeding heart over the sons and sins of men.

Jeremiah, son of Hilkiah, was native to Anathoth, a village about
three miles from Jerusalem, a city appointed for the priests in that area

of Judaea which was allotted to the tribe of Benjamin. Like John the Baptist and the apostle Paul, Jeremiah was ordained from his mother's womb to serve the Lord. Not until about his twentieth year, when he was specifically addressed by the Lord, did he accept that appointment to be prophet both to the Jew and the Gentile. Even then he declined, citing inability and youth; but "influenced by divine encouragement, he obeyed." He continued to prophesy upwards of forty years during several successive reigns of the degenerating successors of King Josiah, to whom he fearlessly and faithfully warned of divine judgment which their vacillating, rebellious and iniquitous conduct would wreak upon them and their nation.

His commission from God meant a ministry that would be contentious—a constant clash with the people and their philosophies. God's call to the prophet commissioned him "over the nations and over the kingdoms, to root out, and to pull down, and to destroy, and to throw down, to build, and to plant" (1:10). As the nation decayed and deteriorated in morality and spirituality, Jeremiah's entreaties and prophecies that sought to draw both "hearts and imaginations" of the people from their alliances with the kingdoms about them and from their iniquitous and incorrigible spirit brought him imprisonment and maltreatment as no other man of Israel's prophetic office ever suffered.

Many personal circumstances from his life are interwoven into the text of his prophecies. Contemplating the calamitous consequences of Israel's sins, Jeremiah, in most vivid, descriptive terms and under most express imaginations, defined the desecration the invading enemy would inflict. "At one time we hear him groaning over his text as he stands beside the potter at his wheel, while the potter mars his vessel and casts it away. At the River Euphrates he prepares a message to preach as he sees in the sands the footprints of his captive people." Another time he dashes an earthen vessel to pieces before the eyes of his amazed and enraged congregation of elders. To challenge a false prophet's preaching, "Peace when there is no peace," Jeremiah appeared before his people with his neck in a yoke of wood. Sometimes his messages were ignored; more times they incensed the people; one was incendiary—King Jehoiakim burned the roll of the prophecies uttered against Israel and Judah.

Jeremiah's prophecies were of most illustrious character. He foretold the fate of kings: Shallum, Jehoiakim, Coniah and Zedekiah. He was first to witness and warn of the Babylonian captivity, the precise time of its duration and the return of the Jews to Jerusalem. He described in detail the destruction of Babylon and the downfall of a host of nations. "He foreshadowed the miraculous conception of

Christ, the virtue of His atonement, the spiritual character of His covenant, the inward efficacy of His laws."[2]

Holy zeal fired Jeremiah to write in eloquent tones; a broken heart prompted him to write in tenderest tones; and the urgency of the times provoked him to write in simplest tones. Mentioned J. C. Morgan: "In the story of Jeremiah shrinking in pain and tears we have a picture of a man in such fellowship with God that through him God was able to reveal His own suffering in the presence of sin."

Chapters 31 and 33 of Jeremiah and the Book of Lamentations bare the heart of the prophet most clearly. "There is nothing in all the Scriptures so eloquent of love and sorrow and consolation as the 31st and 33rd chapters of Jeremiah. No words can be found in any language of such touching beauty as all that strain."[3]

Lamentations was written after the manner of the funeral odes, some suggest after the death of King Josiah. But a greater desolation, death and destruction are witnessed in that writing: the destruction of Jerusalem, the captivity of Judah, the demise of the worship of Jehovah, the doom that Deity had determined upon His people who had rejected Him. Pathos pours from Jeremiah's poem, divided into five parts, distributed in twenty-two stanzas corresponding with the twenty-two letters of the Hebrew alphabet, and tripled to sixty-six stanzas in chapter 3.

"The poem affords the most elegant variety of striking scenes that ever probably was displayed in so small a compass ... the circumstances of calamaities resulting in the most affecting picture of desolation and misery," well wrote one writer.

Read Jeremiah's prophecy and his lamentations. Weep with him and realize that our beloved nation of America is headed heedlessly and hopelessly toward a similar visitation of judgment from the sin-angered and sin-avenging Almighty God.

Jeremiah never married in obedience to divine decree. "Of such sensibility, spirituality, sympathy and melancholy," Whyte wrote, "all that a sensitive and melancholy minister takes home and tells only to his wife—all that Jeremiah took and told to God, till his book before us is one long confidence and conversation, one long submission, and silence and surrender and service to God."[4]

Aye, again, small wonder Christ's disciples—knowing of Jeremiah's "suffering sympathy both with God and men, his unretaliating forbearance, his yearning concern for his fellows—his diligence for self-sacrifice, and his utter faithfulness even to the point of unsparing severity in denunciation"[5] when asked by Christ, "Whom do men say that I am?" honestly and humbly answered, "Jeremiah."

NOTES:

1. Alexander Whyte, *Whyte's Bible Characters* (Grand Rapids: Zondervan Publishing House, 1975), p. 395.
2. Ibid., p. 400.
3. Ibid., p. 398.
4. Ibid., p. 401.
5. Ibid., p. 400.

Jonah

The Unwilling Evangelist

Scripture has few if any equals to the sad, shameful story of the first evangelist to the Gentiles—the prophet Jonah. Enigmatic. Egoist. How could one adequately describe this merciless man who so flagrantly sinned against the mission given him by God? Jonah's sin is the dastardly deed of the derelict doctor who refuses to go and minister to a dying patient; the infamous iniquity of the firemen who hear but refuse to heed the clarion call to a flaming home. Again, Jonah's crime is the crime of the citizen who refuses to answer the call to arms by his country upon attack by the enemy. And it is the same capital crime of the Christian who disobeys divine summons to go and seek the unsaved in earnest effort to win them to Christ.

Jonah's story is well-known. Called by God to prophesy against the sinful Assyrian city of Nineveh, Jonah not only refused to obey his Lord, he sought to run away from God. Jonah, of course, believed he had realistic reason for his reluctance and refusal to go to Nineveh. An intensely patriotic Jew, Jonah was justifiably fearful that the Ninevites, sworn and strong enemies of Israel, would repent at his message. Knowing "that thou art a gracious God, and merciful, slow to anger, and of great kindness, and repentest thee of the evil" (Jonah 4:2), Jonah refrained to go to Nineveh and ran off to Tarshish (Spain), convinced God would not destroy the Ninevites if they repented!

Jonah shortly discovered what every sinner or saint who seeks to flee from the presence of the Lord soon shockingly discovers: no sea is wide enough, no transportation fast enough, no day long enough, no night dark enough to escape the pursuing, sin-avenging God.

The reader is doubtlessly well acquainted with the next chapter that comprises the autobiography of this perverse prophet: God exposed His evangelist's disobedience by unleashing a violent storm that struck fear into every seaman's heart and destined that ship to destruction in the surging sea. Jonah confessed his guilt and, knowing the only way to placate that perilous deep was to be cast into it, offered himself a sacrifice to save the sailors' lives. I do not believe that Jonah, in the wildest stretch of his imagination, dreamed that God would prepare a great fish to swallow him alive, spare his life three days and then spew him upon the shores near Nineveh that he might have a second chance to obey God's command.

It has been a much maligned miracle, probably the most abused and unbelieved miracle of the Bible. Yet the notable miracle was not so much that a man would be swallowed by a great fish and that he would be preserved to preach; aye, the greatest miracle was not the "resurrection" account of Jonah—but the repentance and revival of the Ninevites.

Nineveh was then the great Gentile city of the world. Its population numbered 120,000 preschool children (4:11). It was a city which had been built by winning great wars; a city with great walls built for protection; a city wealthy; but a city wicked, wanton, iniquitous, idolatrous and impious.

Into this sprawling metropolis Jonah came to preach. God's grace had given him a second chance. After his experience in the sea, though smelling something of fish, Jonah must have ministered as a man made alive from the dead. One writer witnessed, "His face doubtless shone, like Moses', with the glory of God; his eye flashed, his brow was knit, and his lips trembled as he shouted, 'Yet forty days, and Nineveh shall be overthrown!' "[1] I believe it.

His message was short (actually only five Hebrew words), simple, stern, solemn, imperious, vindictive, hope-dispelling, doom-insuring:

"Yet forty days, and Nineveh shall be overthrown!" Jonah's message definitely was not deemed nor disputed to be the idle, insane words of some religious quack. His warning was accepted as an ultimatum from Heaven. Ninevites, from king to commoner, heard, believed, repented and hoped, appealing to this one argument, "Who can tell if God will turn and repent, and turn away from his fierce anger, that we perish not?" (3:9).

That God did hear and honor their repentance with revival and restoration is sacred history. But God's sparing of the city resulted also in a pouting, pained prophet who incredibly petitioned God that he might die!

> [Jonah] was vexed, not because he felt discredited in the eyes of the men of Nineveh, or because his professional standing as a prophet was ruined by the failure of his prediction, but because of God's clemency toward Nineveh; being willing to spare a city which would only continue to harass and decimate Israel through war and the exaction of heavier and ever heavier tribute. In short, Jonah was vexed because of a narrow, selfish patriotism with which he was obsessed. . . . In his despondency Jonah resembles Elijah, (1 Kings 19:1-18). But there was a difference between them. . . as G. H. Smith has pointed out . . . "Elijah was jealous *for* God; Jonah was jealous *of* God"[2]

Bless God—He not only showered mercy upon the undeserving Ninevites; he showed the same magnanimous mercy to His unprofitable prophet. As Jonah sat in seclusion under a scorching sky, sullen, still desirous of the city's destruction, the Lord prepared "with almost magical swiftness, a bottle-gourd"[3] to shield and succor His pouting prophet. For a season the prophet was pleased. But, just as swiftly, God prepared a worm to gnaw upon the gourd and wither it to the ground. Jonah became more embittered against his God. "He had been angry, at first, because Nineveh *was spared;* he is now angry because the gourd *was not spared.*"[4]

In Jonah 4:10 and 11, God lays bare His burdened heart to His hard-hearted prophet. The passage is a high-water mark of the Old Testament, often cited as the Old Testament counterpart to John 3:16, "For God so loved the world. . . ." In this timeless text, a truth far in advance of Jonah's age, God expresses His definition of evangelism that the whole, wide world hear the gospel; the trenchant truth that the throb of God's heart was not that the Jewish nation only hear and hold the knowledge of the one true God, Jehovah, and His love for the lost, but that all—Gentiles as well as Jews, Ninevites as well as Jerusalemites—hear of the amazing, saving, forgiving grace of God. Thus to a small-souled, nationalistic, bigoted prophet, God pleads:

Then said the LORD, Thou hast had pity on the gourd, for the which thou hast not laboured, neither madest it grow; which came up in a night, and perished in a night: And should not I spare Nineveh, that great city, wherein are more than sixscore thousand persons that cannot discern between their right hand and their left hand?

What more can or should be added than the paraphrase of the poet: "Lord, take my feet and make them move—At the impulse of thy love!"

NOTES:

1. Robinson, *The Twelve Minor Prophets,* p. 8.
2. Ibid., pp. 73, 74.
3. Ibid.
4. Ibid.

Josiah

Youth Aflame for God

A youth on fire for God is not necessarily the norm in the teenage set. Youth, even Christian youth, are more characterized by instability than stability; indecision rather than decisiveness; lukewarmness instead of hot heartedness. In this they very much emulate their elders.

Josiah was an exciting exception to the rule. He came on the scene a scintillating star, roared through life a blazing comet, finally to be burned out in a premature death. "Josiah was the one bright light in the last 100 years of Israel's history," J. G. Greenough gauged, further judging, "Josiah broke a long monotonous series of absolutely

61

worthless monarchs. Before him and behind him were moral waste and darkness. He stands out as a figure worth looking at and loving . . . Josiah's good reign was like a burst of brilliant sunset, before the final darkness comes on."[1]

Josiah was just eight years of age when he ascended the throne to become king. The times were terrifying. Josiah's father, Amon, and his grandfather, Manasseh, had led Judah into a total departure from God, until the nation was tragically debased and degraded, living in grossest immoralities and idolatries. The kingdom was divided; civil war was being waged; violence and villainies filled the land. It was an apostate nation, destined for destruction. In those horror, hopeless hours Jeremiah was tearfully yet fearlessly prophesying sure, soon judgment from the holy God of Heaven. It was an hour that would test the most spiritually souled, mature minded, trained-for-his task kind of a king. But in the sovereignty and economy of God, a child of our present-day third grade school system became monarch.

Josiah had some bad men in his parentage, but God gave him a great mother, Jedidah, and a great pastor, Jeremiah. Alexander Whyte witnessed, "With Jeremiah every Sabbath day among the ruins of the temple, and with Jedidah every weekday at home, notwithstanding Josiah's drawbacks and heartbreaks—or, rather because of them—I do not wonder that Josiah became the best sovereign that ever sat upon the throne of David."[2] Whyte's evaluation has scriptural support, for they state of Josiah: "And like unto him was there no king before him, that turned to the LORD with all his heart, and with all his soul, and with all his might, according to the law of Moses; neither after him arose there any like him" (2 Kings 23:25).

As an eight-year-old, Josiah set his heart to seek the Lord, the God of his "father" David. As Dr. Whyte also wrote:

> However well a boy may have been brought up; however good a mother a boy may have had, and however faithful and efficient a minister, the time soon comes when every young man must seek his own God for himself. Neither David's God, nor Jedidah's God, nor Jeremiah's God will suffice for Josiah. . . . He must be able to say for himself, 'Thou art my God. Early will I seek thee. O Lord, truly I am thy servant. . . .' "[3]

Such kindred relationship and fellowship with the thrice holy God kindled a fervency in Josiah's young soul to totally serve his God and to totally exterminate the moral and spiritual corruption in his nation. Thus, a preteenaged boy, the same age as our Little League ball players, poured out his life's blood into purging his land of evil!

Reformation began on a low level at first, but by the time Josiah was twelve years of age, his sin-enraged spirit set out to sweep idolatry out of his kingdom. Images of Ashtoreth and altars of Baalim were broken down. Even the bones of the priests buried there were burned upon the heaps, thus desecrating them so that they could never be used again as a seat of sacrifice.

By the time Josiah was twenty, his reformation was in full scale. As suggested by historians, Josiah's reformation of religion was as radical and far-reaching as any launched by a Luther, a John Knox or a Calvin, but with this distinct difference:

> Those great European reformers had the whole of the Word of God in their hands both to inspire them and to guide and support them in their tremendous task. But Josiah had not one single book or chapter or verse of the Word of God in his heathen day . . . the whole of that immense movement that resulted in the religious regeneration of Jerusalem and Judah of Josiah's day—it all sprang originally and immediately out of nothing else but Josiah's tenderness of heart.[4]

Reformation led to rebuilding. Altars were demolished; groves were destroyed; idolatrous priests and people were demoted, defeated by the young monarch. But Josiah knew that simply purging a land would not purify its people. So when he was about twenty-six years of age, Josiah set in motion the task of rebuilding the Temple and restoring worship of the true and living Lord Jehovah.

Forty years that Temple had lain in ruins. In the rubble and rubbish of the ruins of that holy house, possibly in the very holy of holies room, Hilkiah the priest uncovered an amazing sight: a long-lost book—the book of the Law given by God to Moses. Those Scriptures were read to Josiah. Some students of Scripture suggest it was possibly the reading of Deuteronomy 27 and 28, chapters which contain the curses that would be leveled by the Lord upon the land if His people forsook that law. Those precise pages startled the zealous Josiah to realize how jealous Jehovah was of His holy name.

Convicted over the grave pronouncements, conscious of the greatness of the sins of his people, concerned as to the possible destruction of his kingdom because of God's pent up wrath, Josiah rose from his throne, rent his clothes and requested Huldah the prophetess. Why he called for Huldah rather than Jeremiah, who had to be Josiah's greatest source of spiritual purpose and power, is not shown in the Scripture. However, Huldah had a message from Heaven! She assured the king that judgment on Judah was inevitable and it was also imminent. But some blessed words fell upon the earnest king's ears:

And as for the king of Judah, who sent you to enquire of the LORD, so shall ye say unto him, Thus saith the LORD God of Israel concerning the words which thou hast heard; Because thine heart was tender, and thou didst humble thyself before God, when thou heardest his words against this place, and against the inhabitants thereof, and humbledst thyself before me, and didst rend thy clothes, and weep before me; I have even heard thee also, saith the LORD. Behold, I will gather thee to thy fathers, and thou shalt be gathered to thy grave in peace, neither shall thine eyes see all the evil that I will bring upon this place (2 Chron. 34:26-28).

Huldah's message from Heaven incited Josiah to more feverish efforts and energies toward revival. He summoned the religious leaders and had that newly discovered law of Moses—its commands and curses—read to them. He appealed to them to reconfirm the covenant which the elders had broken. B. H. Carroll commented:

> This was an epoch in the life of Josiah and of the nation and in the life of Jeremiah also, for we find in Jeremiah 11 that it had great effect on his preaching. He had been prophesying several years before this, and in chapter 11 his preaching took a new turn: "Thus saith the LORD, Hear ye the words of his covenant, and speak unto the men of Judah, and to the inhabitants of Jerusalem."[5]

Jeremiah had a new text—the renewed covenant. Josiah had a renewed task—complete his reformation. Thus he cleansed the Temple of all vessels dedicated to Baal, to Ashtereth, to the hosts of Heaven. He "brake down the houses of the sodomites" where they carried on their abominations under the name of religion. He removed the idolatrous priests from the Temple and from the high places. He, as King Hezekiah had done years earlier, defiled Topheth, where sons had been cruelly sacrificed in the fiery arms of Molech. He destroyed the horses the kings of Judah had made as offerings to the sun. Josiah's intensity to abolish idolatry inspired him to go even into the northern kingdom (Samaria) to destroy altars to idols, chiefly the altars of Bethel. The annihilation of that altar of atrocities in defiance of the Lord God fulfilled the pointed prophecy of the old unnamed man of God against the altar of King Jeroboam (1 Kings 13:1-3). The Passover was reinstituted, observed with such splendor that the Scriptures state of it, "And there was no passover like to that kept in Israel from the days of Samuel" (2 Chron. 35:18).

But with all of Josiah's reforms, with all the consent, the conformity of the elders and people in confirming the covenant and keeping the Passover, there was no real revival! Theirs was only an outward reform, an outward repentance, mere mental agreement and acceptance. There was no inward response, return or revival. Josiah, who turned to the Lord as a youth with all his heart, and who served the Lord all his years with all his might, and who was revered in the chronicles of the kings of Judah by Jeremiah as the noblest of all her kings, could not change his people's hearts!

Nor could Jeremiah, with all his authoritative, Heaven-born preaching and prophesying, with all his tears shed over his corrupt congregation, move the hearts of the people. The moral sense of the people had become so blurred, so insensible to sin, it was difficult, aye, nigh unto impossible, to respond wholly to the king's and the prophet's commands and leadership.

> Through prophet after prophet and providence after providence God had pleaded with His people, but they had repeatedly shown that they "*would* not," until now, by that deadly process which ever operates in human nature, they had reached the point where they *could* not. Apostasy and idolatry had now become ingrained in the national character.[6]

At the age of thirty-nine Josiah died. Death is always too imminent, too ironic, too inexpedient. Josiah's death was also incredibly strange. Why he would enter into a war Assyria was waging against Egypt was strange indeed. It had to be a presumptuous, political venture. Possibly his great spiritual successes provoked a pride in Josiah in which he presumed God would grant him similar successes in the military theaters too. The sin of presumption is a suicidal sin. Josiah armed himself and disguised himself; nonetheless, he was mortally wounded in the battle at Meggiddo.

The hour Josiah expired on the plains of Armageddon, the lights went out on the nation of Judah. Their king, a flame for righteousness and revival from his youth, a burning and shining light in a darkened, degenerate nation, had just been extinguished. No other such king was on the horizon. Josiah truly had been "the last burst of a brilliant sunset, before the darkness comes on." Next was the Babylonian army besieging Jerusalem, beating down its walls, burning the city, butchering its people, bearing the exiles into a strange land.

NOTES:

1. Herbert Lockyer, *All the Men of the Bible* (Grand Rapids: Zondervan Publishing House, 1958), p. 207.
2. Whyte, *Whyte's Bible Characters*, p. 357.
3. Ibid., p. 356.
4. Ibid.
5. Carroll, *An Interpretation of the English Bible,* 2:194.
6. J. Sidlow Baxter, *Explore the Book,* 6 vols. (Grand Rapids: Zondervan Publishing House, 1960), 2:150.

Nehemiah

Spiritual Leadership

He called himself "Tirshatha," the boss. Hebrew history heralds him as one of its illustrious sons. I list him as one of the greatest examples of spiritual leadership. Nehemiah was not a prophet, not a priest, not a preacher. He was a patriot, but more than that he was a prince, not a royal-born prince, but a prince among men. He is one of the Bible's highest and holiest examples of lay leadership.

Nehemiah was another of those Jewish heroes in their humbled hour of the Babylonian-Persian captivity. Along with Daniel, Ezra and others, he was an exiled Jew in a foreign land because the sins of prior generations of Jewish parents and priests had provoked God's wrath and justice to judgment upon His people. A remnant of Jews under

Ezra and others in fulfillment of Jeremiah's and Daniel's prophecies had returned to Jerusalem. The Temple had been restored in some measure, and Jews were living again in the semi-renovated city. But the walls, gates and towers still lay in ruins, the result of that Babylonian devastation nearly a century before.

Nehemiah, patriot that he was, knew well that the walls and battlements of a city in those times signified not only the security of a city but also symbolically told its testimony. The rubble and ruins sounded eloquently the impending, imminent danger of the total destruction of the unfortified, defenseless city. But those same ruins also told in melancholy tones the abject poverty of the restored remnant and their evident indifference and idleness to rebuild the ruins. Worst of all, they told the total absence of the prosperity and glory of God upon His people.

Thus Nehemiah's autobiography begins with a portrait of his own melancholy mien. Cupbearer to the king, a position that involved more than mere servitude, Nehemiah was in actuality a confidant to the king. He was acquainted with the diplomacy, the dispatch and decisions of the king's court. Through his brother Hanani, Nehemiah had learned of the lamentable conditions of Jerusalem. He had been stricken to pray and fast, confessing his sins and the sins of his people, petitioning God that those calamitous conditions might be corrected. It is evident in those months of entreaty to God that the Lord laid upon Nehemiah's heart the burden of rebuilding the walls. It is also evident that the affliction of his people affected him physically. Eventually he could not conceal his concern. Thus one day a sad-faced cupbearer served his king. Artaxerxes, the king, thus became aware of Nehemiah's grieved spirit, and queried him for the reason, at the same moment volunteering his assistance.

Those months of petitioning Heaven not only moved the king's heart (Prov. 21:1); they also had molded and matured in Nehemiah's mind the full program he must pursue and the petition he should ask the king when opportunity came. Nehemiah's request was staggering. He wanted leave to go to Jerusalem, letters to authorities en route to insure protection, and largess to rebuild the walls. Such a bold request could have occasioned Nehemiah's death; rather, under God, it opened the treasuries of the palace and the door to Nehemiah's deliverance!

Nehemiah, his manpower and materials arrived safely in Jerusalem. B. H. Carroll commented upon that arrival:

When he reached Jerusalem he found matters to the last degree desperate and deplorable. Outside of the almost irrepairable internal disaster, he found the mongrel Samaritans allied with Israel's ancient enemies. This coalition not only rejoiced in the downfall of Jerusalem but also conspired to perpetuate its desolation. So vigilant were their efforts against its restoration and so watchful of him that Nehemiah had to survey the ruins by candlelight at night![1]

It is a sad scene in Scripture when we walk with Nehemiah through those ruins and watch him weep over the shattered, stark scene. Nehemiah may well have been the first man to weep in that solitary city since Jeremiah had sobbed out his sorrows a century earlier.

Undaunted, Nehemiah organized his forces. Fathers, sons, mothers, daughters were all drafted for the task. Understand opposition to Nehemiah, his person and program were also organized, and that opposition intensified. Nehemiah and his workers were insulted, impugned, dared, defied, resisted, wronged. But one of history's greatest engineering, building programs was accomplished in fifty-two days!

The *scorn* heaped upon Nehemiah and his builders was silenced by Nehemiah's trust in God and His promises. "God . . . will prosper us . . . ye have no portion, nor right, nor memorial, in Jerusalem" (2:20). *Ridicule* was returned upon the heads and hearts of the enemy by Nehemiah's prayers that that reproach would fall in retribution on the heads of the accusers—which it did (4:4-6)! The enemies' *threatenings* to attack and destroy were thwarted by Nehemiah when he set up a 24-hour-a-day watch. Builders used both sword and trowels (4:18). It was sleepless vigilance and diligence. Treachery in attempts to sidetrack the work were turned away by Nehemiah's sense of priorities. *Accusations* were aborted. Nehemiah set the facts straight before both foes and friends (6:5-9). An *attempt* to assassinate Nehemiah was aborted (6:10-14).

Not altogether incredible (it seems situations in our churches today are significantly, shamefully similar), Nehemiah's leadership also had to be lent to eliminating grave internal corruptions—the evils of the religious, returning remnant. The offenders were elders, nobles, rulers. Again, Nehemiah had to become the Tirshatha. Those who labored with him rebuilding the walls were for the most part poverty-stricken people. Living in penury, they were at the same time incredibly in bondage to the religious leaders. Their homes, their land, aye, oftentimes their children had been mortgaged to ruthless, greedy rulers who had levied upon the mortgagees interest or usury at an impossible-to-pay, illegal rate of 12 percent. In their misery they revealed this inequity to Nehemiah. In one of Scripture's humorous if not so tragic scenes, Nehemiah "shook [his] lap, and said, So God shake out every man from his house" who does not restore the properties to their rightful owners and release the oppressed from the illegal interest. Suffice it to say, those wrongs were righted. Then spirit was rekindled, workers united, the task completed, "for the people had a mind to work."

It had to be one of Nehemiah's holiest, happiest, hallelujah hours when he and Ezra, the priest, led the people to the dedication of the finished walls. Jerusalem again was the city of Jehovah, fortified by men and blessed by God.

Nehemiah's labors for his Lord did not cease. A city had been fortified, its citizens united, but the people's morals and spirituality had eroded in the seven decades of deportation. A revival was sorely needed! The Ammonites and Moabites had intermingled then intermarried with the returned remnant. A separated people, called to holiness, had corrupted and polluted themselves. Even Tobiah, the hated enemy of the rebuilding of the walls, had been given a place of authority and access into the very Temple of God, even into the treasury room! Tirshatha took charge, casting Tobiah out of the Temple, then cleansing that house of God of its every impurity. Levites, who had suffered want financially and physically since their return, had their needs supplied by Nehemiah, who contended with the rulers: "Why is the house of God forsaken?"

Sabbath breaking, a crime that had caused the Jews deportation, became again a profane practice. Nehemiah dealt severely with the Sabbath breakers, first warning them of God's will and wrath upon disobedience, then threatening violators with physical force. "If ye do so again, I will lay my hands upon you!" Those alien marriages were dealt with by a man concerned that his people be holy people. Earlier, Ezra, the priest, had wept as he pled with offenders to repent of their sin and forsake their alien wives. Nehemiah was much more vocal and visual. He called them to him, cursed them, plucked off his beard, literally chased away one priest who had married a heathen wife. His tactics triumphed. A reformation followed. The priesthood which had become polluted was purged. A confession of sin was made into a covenant and signed and sealed by the religious leaders. The ordinance of the firstfruits was observed again. Once more Judah was entrenched in their homeland, fortified in their holy city, obedient to the law of their God.

One man had mightily brought about much of this restoration and revival. Nehemiah's great leadership had prevailed over a downtrodden, discouraged, decadent people. His fearlessness had nerved his fearful people to fearlessness. His patriotism and spirituality had rallied them to rebuild the fallen, feeble ruins. His dedication, devotion and diligence had fired them to persist against seeming impossible odds. His tireless example rallied all rich and poor, men and women, peasant and prince to unite, persist, work, war and win! That is why the walls were rebuilt!

His fervent prayer life (read that soul-searching, sin-confessing, revival-throbbing prayer in chapter 9); his burning heart of holiness and righteousness; his sterling character; his unselfishness with his own wealth; his shining example of total, humble dependence upon his God endeared him to his people; exerted them to repentance; and wrought a great reformation and a return to God's laws by a once great people who had returned home from seven decades of servitude only to discover themselves disorganized, still terribly depraved and totally disunited and altogether disinterested in doing anything about it.

The need of that hour was a great spiritual leader. Nehemiah was the man! Tirshatha, he could boss because he was a prince with God and a prince to his people! Need I add, this is the need of the hour in countless Christian homes and in countless fundamental churches and in countless halls of congress, senates, state houses and the White House!

NOTE:

1. B. H. Carroll, *Evangelistic Sermons* (Westwood, NJ: Fleming H. Revell Co., 1913), p. 115.

Samuel

Circuit-Riding Preacher

There have been giants in the history of the Jews. Many, indeed, are the illustrious worthies who have contributed to the spiritual life of that nation. Standing head and shoulders among the people of his generation was Samuel. Many-faceted was his ministry, for he was at once a priest, a judge, a prophet, a teacher and a circuit preacher.

Every Sunday school pupil will remember the story of Samuel's birth in answer to the prevailing prayer of the childless Hannah and her subsequent lending of her lad to the Lord. First, he served the priest Eli in the temple of the Lord until Eli's tragic death. Those were dark, desperate days in Israel's history. The hated Philistine nation had conquered Israel and had made them bondslaves. The Ark of the

Covenant (the symbol of God's presence, provision and protection) had been captured by the enemy. Like America today, in Israel, according to the Scriptures, man did that which was right in his own eyes. Violence, villainy and vice filled the land. The priests were profane; the people profligate. It was a day of spiritual and moral famine. Well had Eli's daughter-in-law named her son Ichabod—"the glory of the Lord has departed." Defeat, discouragement, despair and doom, like a pall, had settled over the land. Eli and his sons had been judged for their sins. It was evident that a national judgment would fall next. This was the situation Samuel surveyed when he assumed the office of priest upon the death of Eli.

Samuel had believed God's time of deliverance was nigh. He called the representatives of Israel together, challenging them, "If ye do return unto the LORD with all your hearts, then put away the strange gods and Ashtaroth from among you, and prepare your hearts unto the LORD, and serve him only: and he will deliver you out of the hand of the Philistines" (1 Sam. 7:3). His hope-bringing message was heard and heeded. The people came to Mizpeh to meet him so that he might pray for them. There they confessed their sins, calling upon the name of the Lord. Revival fires were lit. When the word of this "revolt" reached the ears of the Philistine leaders, their army was dispatched immediately to check this revival. *But God intervened!* He sent a terrible thunderstorm that confounded the Philistine army, confused their ranks and scattered their forces. The Israelites pursued the fleeing Philistines and conquered them. The Philistines were never a force again in the days of Samuel. God gave peace to the land all his days.

Samuel was doubtlessly the first circuit-riding preacher in history, for the Lord witnesses, "And he went from year to year in circuit to Beth-el, and Gilgal, and Mizpeh, and judged Israel in all those places" (1 Sam. 7:16).

But he did more than preach to the people. Samuel was a great teacher in Israel. By his life of prevailing, persistent prayers; by the moral greatness of his character; by his tireless tramping from city to city to teach righteousness and revival to the elders and to that group of impressionable, plastic hearts and minds of youth; Samuel was the one man, among all other men, who was the saving and sanctifying power that steered the nation of Israel away from the apostasy and anarchy for a whole generation in one of that nation's darkest and deepest hours of its history. This group of youth, by the way, became the school or "college of the prophets," and was to include such worthies as Elijah and Elisha.

Terribly, tragically, Samuel's own sons failed their father, forsaking his ways in following the Lord, and added to the demand of Israel to desire a king like all the nations.

Their desire and demand for a monarchy was an insult to the man Samuel and his ministry and an insurrection against God and His theocracy. But in obedience to God's command, Samuel anointed Saul to be king. Later he anointed David. Doubtlessly he did not live long after anointing David to be king.

His death was the cause of great lament. Israel lost *something* and *someone* when Samuel died, and they knew it, for the Scripture states: "And Samuel died; and all the Israelites were gathered together, and lamented him, and buried him in his house at Ramah" (1 Sam. 25:1). Josephus commented:

> He was a man whom the Hebrews honoured in an extraordinary degree: for that lamentation which the people made for him, and this during a long time, manifested his virtue, and the affection which the people bore for him; as also did the solemnity and concern that appeared about his funeral. . . . They buried him in his own city of Ramah; and wept for him a very great number of days. . . .[1]

But the greatest commentary on the character of a man who served his God and his people in the interest of revival and righteousness are the words of the nation to his appeal near the close of his life. Samuel's question was:

> I am old and grayheaded; and, behold, my sons are with you: and I have walked before you from my childhood unto this day. Behold, here I am: witness against me before the LORD, and before his anointed: whose ox have I taken? or whose ass have I taken? or whom have I defrauded? whom have I oppressed? or of whose hand have I received any bribe to blind mine eyes therewith? and I will restore it to you" (1 Sam. 12:2, 3).

Their answer spoke of a man whose life was sterling, shining in its spirituality: "Thou hast not defrauded us, nor oppressed us, neither hast thou taken ought of any man's hand" (1 Sam. 12:4).

A study of the man Samuel, his ministry, his spirituality, his power with God, his power with men, his purposes and his passions leaves us with a feeling of littleness, but I trust with a deepened desire—*more of the same kind of prayer and the same kind of purity!*

NOTE:

1. William Whiston, trans., *The Life and Work of Flavius Josephus* (Philadelphia: The John C. Winston Co., n.d.), p. 196.

Ananias

Church-Caller Who Changed History

Meet one of Christian history's unheralded heroes—an amazing man by the name of Ananias. Little has been written about this man, but he made one of the most important visits ever made. Acts 9:10-19 recounts that visit which, under God, turned the whole course of church history.

I was shocked to discover that in my well-stocked biographical library I had only two volumes that make more than mere mention of the man. And in my full files of magazines, articles and papers, I had nothing about the centuries-spanning, shining example of one of Heaven's most illustrious personal workers. I should not have been so surprised because the Scriptures speak only sparingly of Ananias and his achievements. Acts 9 and 22 have precisely 437 words about this man and his mission when he led Saul (the apostle Paul) into assurance of his salvation.

74

The Scripture's scant reference to this elite evangelist is not unique. Such lack of biographical information on soul-winners who have led illustrious converts to Christ is the rule rather than the exception. Who can cite the name of the soul-winning Sunday school teacher who led D. L. Moody to Christ? How about the identity of the lay preacher whose sermon and personal plea to a young hearer were responsible for the salvation of Spurgeon's soul? Who were the sidewalk evangelists who caused Billy Sunday to be the curbstone recruit for Christ? Even more recently, name the Sunday school teacher who led Lee Roberson to Christ.

I believe you see the principle. Examples of similar evangelism by individuals whose names have been unnoticed and unrecorded are numerous. At least in the account of Paul's conversion we do learn the soul-winner's name. And in those brief sentences of Scripture, we see some of the great spiritual strengths of a man of God used by God in one of evangelism's most extraordinary episodes!

Again, as is usually the case, Deity depended upon a disciple to reach a soul for the Savior. The disciple in this instance was Ananias—an unheralded, unknown, "unimportant" Christian living in Damascus. The Scriptures speak of him simply as "a certain disciple," suggesting he was a common kind of Christian, one without rank, authority of an apostle, or the power and position of a pastor or preacher. As Dr. Sidlow Baxter suggested:

> Likely enough we should never have heard anything about him had it not been for his figuring in Paul's conversion. He was just an ordinary, humble disciple who evidently sought to glorify Jesus by a consecrated life amid the unexciting exactness of customary Damascus ways and doings.[1]

It is evident that Ananias was a devoted, dedicated disciple. He was a "devout man according to the law," and he had "a good report of all the Jews which dwelt" in Damascus (Acts 22:12). Ananias, according to that bit of biography, had to be a Damascene, not one of the dispersed Christians who had been driven out of Jerusalem under the persecution of Saul. His testimony to the community had not been built in a few weeks or months. Ananias had lived a clean, clear-cut, consistent witness before believing Christians and unbelieving Jews for a long time, "in season and out of season."

Dr. A. C. Gaebelein grants that Ananias was doubtlessly the leader of the Christian assembly in Damascus.[2] If such be the case, the soul that he was to reach for Christ would be the man whose fury and hatred had been aimed at Ananias, the antagonist of Saul of Tarsus!

Aye, Saul of Tarsus! He was the Christ-hating, Christian-killing, church-persecuting Saul of Tarsus. His very name filled the hearts of Christ's faithful followers with fear. Acts 8:3 records of that satanically-inspired, frantic and fanatic rebel: "As for Saul, he made havock of the church, entering into every house, and haling men and women committed them to prison."

Armed with an arsenal of authority from the priests of Jerusalem, Saul was en route to Damascus to seize the saints of that city, slay them or incarcerate them in the insult, the indecencies of imprisonment. Ananias was one of those marked men!

But the Word of God witnesses that outside the Damascus city limits God struck down that rebellious, zealous, murderous sinner. Blinded, broken and repentant, the once boasting, blatant, unbelieving Pharisee, Saul, was led as a helpless, humbled child into the city. For three days he "neither did eat nor drink" (Acts 9:9).

Then God accosted Ananias: "Arise, and go into the street which is called Straight, and enquire in the house of Judas for one called Saul of Tarsus: for, behold, he prayeth" (Acts 9:11). It must have seemed ironic to Saul that the man whom he had set out to find, bind and destroy was God's choice to seek him out instead. Ananias was to find Saul, open his blinded eyes, deliver him into the freedom and forgiveness of the gospel, baptize him, and receive him into the company of Christian faith and fellowship.

It was not as simple as that last paragraph implies. A fearful Ananias flinched at God's command, excusing himself on these grounds: "Lord, I have heard by many of this man, how much evil he hath done to thy saints at Jerusalem: And here he hath authority from the chief priests to bind all that call on thy name" (Acts 9:13, 14).

But the Lord said unto him, "Go thy way" (Acts 9:15). And Ananias obeyed, entered the house and faced the fearsome Saul of Tarsus. He made the call that restored sight to Saul, instructed him, assured him of his saving faith, filled him with the Spirit of God, and inaugurated a ministry that overturned the forces of Hell, enthroned Christ, established churches, and commenced a program of evangelism that has shone through the darkness of the centuries until this present moment.

Thank God for this tender, touching and yet subtly humorous account of Ananias, a disciple once paralyzed by fear, but providentially empowered with a childlike faith and a calm sincerity that conquered Saul of Tarsus. This dear man's obedience ought to encourage us to arise and go our way. "Wherefore lift up the hands which hang down, and the feeble knees; And make straight paths for your feet" (Heb. 12:12, 13).

76

The sweet story of Ananias should inspire us to realize that any and every visit for souls, under God, may well result in life-transforming, yea, history-changing results!

NOTES:

1. J. Sidlow Baxter, *Mark These Men* (Grand Rapids: Zondervan Publishing House, 1960), p. 137.

2. A. C. Gaebelein, *Acts of the Apostles* (New York: Our Hope Publication Office, 1912), p. 177.

Andrew

Apostle of Personal Work

Clovis Chappell called him "Andrew, the Ordinary," citing that Andrew was not "nearly so conspicuous nor so gifted as his bluff brother (Peter), nor was he so gifted as his intimate friends, James and John." And he added, "He was by no means the least among the apostles. There were others more significant than he . . . we cannot but face the fact that Andrew was only ordinary."[1]

But ordinary man that he was, Andrew has been rightly recognized as the "apostle of personal workers." He does not come by that title without real reason. Andrew is seen in the Scriptures only three times. But in each instance he is engaged in dealing with someone in the realm of the spiritual or the soul.

First, the Scriptures show Andrew winning his own brother, Simon Peter, to the Savior. Here is the first example of home missions, and here is the commencement of the chain of evangelism in which the whole Christian movement began!

Doubtlessly, no work is more difficult than witnessing to and winning the lost in one's own family. Arguments abound as to why this is true. Besides the evident timidity to witness to members of the family, there is often either a lackluster testimony, or even worse, a tarnished testimony that turns off lost loved ones from hearing or heeding one's warning witness. But worst of all is the blighting, paralyzing indifference that will not even plead with or pray over lost loved ones!

Andrew had none of these obstacles. Although ordinary in all standards, Andrew, upon his conversion to Christ, was fired with a passion and a purpose that he must persuade Peter to become a Christian too. Peter was a braggart, blaspheming brother, cocky, conceited, hard to conquer. He probably argued, balked, kicked, protested and resisted Andrew's appeal. But if so, the earnest, red-hot, enthused Andrew prevailed. The Scriptures cite his success in these succinct sentences: "He first findeth his own brother Simon, and saith unto him, We have found the Messias, which is, being interpreted, the Christ. And he brought him to Jesus" (John 1:41, 42).

It is evident that Andrew, who had been a fisherman from his boyhood in Bethsaida, not only had a winning way with the fierce fisherman; he was equally effective in winning the confidence of a youth. The incident in reference is the Biblical record of a vast congregation on the hills near the Sea of Galilee. It was evening and the crowd which had thronged there by the thousands was weary and hungry after its long travels and attendance at the ministry and miracles of Christ that afternoon.

When Christ proposed to feed that milling, famishing multitude, Philip protested, pleading the insufficient supply of food and strongly suggested that the Savior "send them away, that they may go . . . into the villages, and buy . . . bread" (Mark 6:36). Poor Philip! He knew there was not much bread, but he did not know how little there actually was. But Andrew did. He reported the presence of a boy with five loaves and two fishes. And at the command of Christ, he brought the boy and his meager meal to Christ. Andrew persuaded his new-found friend to leave his lunch with the Lord, the lunch that in the mighty miracle of Christ met the physical needs of over five thousand.

"Persuaded" has to be the right word, for, as R. G. Lee pointed out: "You don't get what a boy has carried along to eat without putting forth some good reasons." Then he added:

As a lad I went to old Massey school in York county. My mother used to fix me fried apple pies—the half moon sort—and biscuits split open and

79

lined with red fried ham. If a boy attempted to get that from me by persuasion, he would have had to give utterance to more wisdom than Socrates, and would have had to speak in a more eloquent way than Patrick Henry. . . .[2]

It is evident that Andrew had won the lad to an open heart in confidence to himself before he ever won his hands to be opened to Christ's claims and cause. Personal evangelism's persuasion is ever based on that principle.

The last look at Andrew in the Bible story is another picture of personal evangelism. A group of Gentiles was seeking the Savior. They came first to Philip, doubtlessly because his name was Grecian, and said to him, "Sir, we would see Jesus" (John 12:21). Why Philip did not capitalize upon their curiosity or concern is not evident. Perhaps he was provincial in his faith, uncertain or unconcerned that "foreigners" should find faith in Christ. Perhaps Philip was unsure how to introduce the inquisitive to the Lord. In his perplexity Philip had to turn to another—and it was automatic, axiomatic that it be Andrew. Andrew was available, able and had the answers. He knew that "God is no respecter of persons: But in every nation he that feareth him, and worketh righteousness, is accepted with him" (Acts 10:34, 35). So he brought them to Jesus!

Tradition tells that Andrew was martyred in Petrea, a city of Achaia, where, because of his witness for Christ, he was "commanded to be crucified; but to be fastened to the cross with cords, instead of nails, that his death might be more lingering and tedious." But the record also attests of Andrew, "Fastened to the cross, on which he hung two whole days, (he was) teaching and instructing the people . . . being sometimes so weak and faint as scarce to have power of utterance."[3]

That account of Andrew is only tradition. It is not told to be truth, yet I do not find it difficult to accept it as truth, for the Bible account of Andrew was always that he was bringing someone to Jesus! If Andrew was an ordinary Christian, it is my prayer that we may have more of his kind in our churches!

NOTES:

1. Clovis Chappell, *Men That Count* (Garden City, NY: Doubleday, Doran & Co., 1929), p. 82.
2. R. G. Lee, *Rose of Sharon* (Grand Rapids: Zondervan Publishing House, 1947), p. 65.
3. Osmond Tiffany, ed., *Patriarchs and Prophets; Christ and the Apostles* (New York: G. & F. Bill Co., 1860), p. 509.

Apollos

Apostolic Evangelism

The Holy Spirit gives us His appraisal of Apollos in two succinct sentences: He was "a Jew . . . born at Alexandria, an eloquent man, and mighty in the scriptures . . . fervent in the spirit . . ." (Acts 18:24, 25). Ancestry—a Jew! Nationality—Alexandrian of Egypt! Ministry—eloquent evangelist! Intellectually—a mighty mind! Spiritually—fervent! With that one flash of light we get a glimpse of one of the most unusual and used-of-God evangelists of sacred story!

Jews were indeed the early evangelists of the glorious gospel and the grace of God, "the oracles of God" having been committed to that race (Rom. 3:2). A listing of such worthies is a roll call of some of the giants of God in the generations of men: Moses, Samuel, Elijah, Isaiah, Jeremiah, Joel, Habakkuk—Old Testament heroes who thundered the

81

laws, proclaimed the prophecies, indicted the iniquitous nations, rallied the people of God back to repentance and revival! In the early days of the apostolic company and the church, such luminaries as John the Baptist, John, Peter, Paul and Philip leap out of the sacred story as the Scriptures show them heralding the Christ, warning of judgment, filling the cities with their evangelism, shaking the thrones of tyrants, shaping the world's history as they witnessed, warned and won in their conquests for Christ. Apollos must be included in the ranks of those worthy witnesses.

As a Jewish youth he learned the Law of Moses, pored over the prophecies of Isaiah, Jeremiah, Daniel and others. He heard the history of his people and marveled at the ministry of Israel's mightiest men, prophet-like preachers: Samuel, Elijah, John the Baptist. Apollos evidently heard that Elijah-like evangelist and forerunner of Christ. There in Judaea he must have been charmed, charged, challenged by John, for one day he would follow in his ministry and message.

As a youth, Apollos also attended the world-renowned synagogue in Alexandria. There he heard the sacred Scriptures read, expounded, discussed. Apollos' background as a Jewish youth contributed consummately to produce a mind mighty in the Scriptures.

The Spirit also states that he was an Alexandrian. To appreciate the wealth that is in those words, one must read histories of the grandeur, the glory of that superlative city nestled on the Nile River. Alexandria breathed beauty. Its architecture was unparalleled among the nations. Its gorgeous geographical situation was unrivaled. But Alexandria's crowning glory was its reputation as the seat of the world's wisdom. It was at Alexandria the sacred Septuagint was set in its final, finished form. Alexandria housed "the world's renowned library into which had been collected the whole literature of the ancient world, the best of Israel . . . Greece, Rome, Egypt, India."[1] And it was in Alexandria where the great schools of learning were found: Homer, Plato, "where the wealth of the minds of wisdom were read and studied."[2] I am sure the Scriptures suggest with real and revealing purpose the place of Apollos' birth, youth, training—Alexandria!

And the Scriptures state further—he was an eloquent man. Eloquence is defined: "Marked by forceful and fluent expression, vividly or movingly expressive or revealing . . . persuasive." Add to that eloquence of Apollos this cardinal, chief characteristic—fervency, for the Word witnessed, "and being fervent in spirit, he spake and taught diligently."

We had better believe it—few men in the ministry of the gospel in all of human history have had the gifts of God that Apollos possessed:

trained in the Old Testament Scriptures; talented with a matchless intellect; tongued with an unusual eloquence and oratory; throbbing with a blazing zeal for Christ! What more could a man have from Heaven?

But the Spirit of God does not abridge a man's biography. He tells the total truth—and the rest of the text reads: "He spake and taught diligently the things of the Lord, knowing only the baptism of John."

It is immediately evident in the Bible biography of the young Alexandrian who entered Ephesus on a preaching mission that he had only a smattering of Scripture learning. His was a kindergarten knowledge, Apollos evidently never hearing or learning more of the New Testament than the truths John the Baptist had espoused. Boldly, fervently, scholarly and eloquently Apollos preached the exhortations John had so powerfully preached twenty years before at Bethabara beyond Jordan. There appeared to be nothing of Christ's promised return, Pentecost, Holy Spirit filling and fulness, nor other great areas of New Testament teaching in Apollos' message. Such had either been missed or misunderstood by the young zealot in his pedagogy and preparation to preach.

In thrilling tones the Bible opens the next chapter in Apollos' life and labors for the Lord. Imagination may run riot here. One can surmise, speculate, suppose how it all commenced, continued and concluded. But in one single sentence the Scriptures spell out that two disciples of Christ in Ephesus, a man and his wife, Aquila and Priscilla, "took him unto them, and expounded unto him the way of God more perfectly" (Acts 18:26).

Alexander Whyte wrote: "I admire all three so much, that I really do not know which to admire the most, Aquila and Priscilla, in their quite extraordinary wisdom and tact and courage, and especially love; or Apollos in his still more extraordinary humility, modesty, and the mind of Christ"[3]

Small wonder that commentator concluded thusly, for Aquila and Priscilla were tentmakers, weavers of goat hair tentcloth, doubtlessly unlettered disciples of the Lord. But this husband and wife who had opened their home to become the center for the church at Ephesus were not unlettered in the doctrine of Christ. Their witness for Him had extended across the great cities of the world—Rome, Ephesus, Corinth. Grounded in the Word, sensitized by and submitted to the Holy Spirit, they were used of Him to be the seminary professors to complete Apollos' theological training for the ministry.

Another fact is certain. To Apollos' eternal praise, that keen-minded Alexandrian, so vitally versed in the Old Testament

Scriptures, so altogether acquainted with the successes of milling crowds who gathered to hear him preach and the multitudes who responded to the challenge and call of his sin-rebuking, soul-burning, Savior-extolling messages, and the man so excellently endued with "many evidences of the gifts of evangelism," humbled himself before that common couple to become a submissive student to the whole teaching of the Scriptures!

Upon completion of his training under the tutelage of that husband and wife team, Apollos was "disposed to pass into Achaia." It may be that Apollos was embarrassed to continue his ministry at Ephesus because of his doctrinal immaturity in his first association with that city. Regardless of the reason, he felt led of the Lord to leave. Again Aquila and Priscilla came to the assistance of this choice Christian youth. They, along with others, gave him letters and credentials, "exhorting the disciples to receive him."

The Spirit of God sheds further light on that luminary, suggesting: "Who, when he was come, helped them much which had believed through grace: For he mightily convinced the Jews, and that publickly, shewing by the scriptures that Jesus was Christ" (Acts 18:27, 28).

Armed then with the whole arsenal of Scripture artillery, Apollos became one of the first century's preeminent preachers. He swept Corinth with his eloquence and logic in exalting Christ, so much so that hardened, cynical, Christ-hating Jews could not withstand the flaming faggots he flung at their unbelief. Apollos became a great power at Corinth, rising to such ascendency that he became the one man many of the members desired in comparison to such elites as Peter and Paul. That church schism did not negate Paul's appreciation for Apollos. The Bible record reveals Apollos was one of Paul's most trusted friends and companions in the ministry. Martin Luther, among others, accepted Apollos as the author of the Book of Hebrews. It is certain, "few men wielded a greater influence for Christ in his day than did Apollos."

Always add to Apollos' name the Holy Spirit's appraisal of the man: "a Jew . . . born at Alexandria, an eloquent man, and mighty in the scriptures . . . fervent in the spirit."

NOTES:
1. Whyte, *Whyte's Bible Characters*, p. 290.
2. Ibid., p. 287.
3. Ibid.

Barnabas

Mr. Big Heart

His name was actually Joseph. He was a Jew, a descendant of the tribe of Levi, a citizen of the island of Cyprus, a landowner, and the man who became the first apostle to the Gentiles with the apostle Paul. But the Bible always refers to this Joseph as Barnabas, a name given him by the apostles because he was a man with a big heart, "the son of consolation," as the word *Barnabas* is by interpretation.

The big heart of Barnabas is first seen in the Bible story in Acts 4:36 and 37. A great wave of revival had swept over Jerusalem. The church had mushroomed from its meager membership of about 120 to over 3,000 on the Day of Pentecost. Souls were being saved daily and added to the church. Thousands thronged the city from afar to witness the mighty working of God. Multitudes of these were saved, and they stayed in Jerusalem. A great need for food, shelter and other physical necessities was evident. The sacrificial spirit of those early saints to

85

insure the continuance of that revival, as well as care for the needs of the believers, is spelled out in Acts 4:34 and 35, and the bigness of Barnabas specifically in verse 37: "Barnabas . . . having land, sold it, and brought the money, and laid it at the apostles' feet."

Revivals then, as today, cost not only time, talent, tears—but also treasure. And Barnabas was willing to pay all the price for revival and revival results.

The next mention of the man and his ministry is in Acts 9:26 and 27. This time Barnabas' bigness was manifest in matters more than money. We see him mediating for a man: Saul of Tarsus. Saul had been a Christ-hater, a church-persecutor, a Christian-killer. He had purposed to stamp out Christianity. So successful was Saul that the Church had gone underground, and the disciples had scattered everywhere. Saul had set out in hot pursuit of them—all the way to Damascus. But on that Damascus journey Saul was intercepted by Jesus Christ, convicted of his sin and converted to the Lord. He was baptized in Damascus and began boldly preaching Jesus Christ as the Son of God until he was forced to flee from the Jews who sought his life.

The one-time Christian-killer returned to Jerusalem as a Christian convert. Suffice it to say, any attempts to join himself to the disciples aborted because they were afraid of the man they remembered only as their avowed enemy.

Barnabas, however, possessed with spiritual discernment, moral courage and compassion, interceded for Saul with his brethren. The Bible records: "But Barnabas took him, and brought him to the apostles, and declared unto them how he [Saul] had seen the Lord in the way, and that he had spoken to him, and how he had preached boldly at Damascus in the name of Jesus" (Acts 9:27).

Barnabas' intercession introduced to the church its mightiest man of ministry, Paul. Well did Charles R. Brown witness: "And we owe it all to the insight and sympathy of this man Barnabas that Paul was not refused and repulsed by the church at Jerusalem."[1]

Barnabas' spiritual stature is also seen in the Scripture account of Acts 13:2. The perimeter of gospel preaching until the time of this text had been most limited in its locale: Jerusalem, Damascus, Joppa, Antioch. And almost all evangelism had been extended only to the Jew, the notable exception being Simon Peter's preaching to the household of the Roman centurion, Cornelius.

The text tells of a momentous meeting and a momentous message. Out of that prayer meeting at Antioch came the watchword for a worldwide witness for Christ in obedience to Christ's command in

Matthew 28:18-20. The Scriptures spell out the choice of the Holy Spirit and the church to establish evangelism's beachhead in an unevangelized world in these words: "The Holy Ghost said, Separate me Barnabas and Saul for the work whereunto I have called them."

That mission later became marked and marred by a dissension between those two notable and noble disciples. John Mark, nephew to Barnabas who had accompanied them on that first ministry, had defected, deserting the party and program to return home. Later, when a second tour was being planned, Barnabas wanted Mark to accompany them again. Paul refused. As one writer cryptly commented:

> Paul, impatient with hesitation and compromise where principle was involved, cut Mark off from any further participation in that missionary movement. He would not lean twice upon a broken or a bending reed. The young man had put his hand to the plow and then had looked back. He was not fit for the kingdom—he could not enter the field again.

But Barnabas, tender toward Mark, was insistent that he be allowed another attempt. So sharp became the contention, the two elder evangelists parted company. Barnabas "took Mark, and sailed unto Cyprus; And Paul chose Silas, and departed . . . And he went through Syria and Cilicia" (Acts 15:39-41).

That Barnabas' sympathetic stand was sensible is seen in some words penned by Paul years later. Writing to Timothy, Paul told him, "Take Mark, and bring him with thee: for he is profitable to me for the ministry" (2 Tim. 4:11). As Barnabas' big heart believed, Mark matured, mastered his mediocrity and became a minister of the gospel.

The Scriptures are strangely silent about Barnabas after his parting with Paul. Tradition tells that after a winning witness for Christ in many countries, Barnabas was inhumanely beaten to death in Cyprus, a martyr for his Master and Savior. No matter what earth's epitaph of this evangelist may read, Heaven's autograph of Barnabas, the son of consolation, is this: "For he was a good man, and full of the Holy Ghost and of faith: and much people was added unto the Lord" (Acts 11:24). We need more men in the ministry of the Lord today with the same kind of bigness as Barnabas!

NOTE:

1. Charles R. Brown, *These Twelve Men* (New York: The Century Co., 1926), p. 209.

Gadarene

Hometown Evangelist

Three gospel writers record the story of one of humanity's most hopeless cases. I write of that wild man, that wretched man, that wicked man, that maniac of Gadara country in the days of Christ. Matthew's Gospel marked him as "possessed with devils . . . exceeding fierce" (8:28). Mark mentions more. He was "a man with an unclean spirit. . . . no man could bind him. . . . neither could any man tame him. . . . night and day, he was in the mountains, and in the tombs, crying, and cutting himself" (5:2-5). Dr. Luke listed: "A certain man, which had devils long time, and ware no clothes, neither abode in any house. . . . he was kept bound with chains and in fetters; and he brake the bands, and was driven of the devil into the wilderness" (8:27, 29).

Taking these texts totally, terrible truths unfold about that most unfortunate man. He was a *demoniac* man. The "legion" of devils possessing him suggest a staggering sum of 2,000 denizens from Hell dominating his entire being! He was a *defiled* man, the Scriptures citing he was possessed of "unclean spirits."

He was a man *dwelling* in the tombs. Graveyards of Christ's day were not the manicured, decorated, aesthetic garden spots we know cemeteries to be today. They were usually caves dug into the sides of hills, and "made hiding places for those who prefer to seek those neglected and commonly out of the way spots and live among the dead." Dr. John Nevius, forty years a missionary to the Chinese, told that in China the demon possessed sought out burial places and established their dwellings there. "It is suggested, and yet a strange fact, that certain forms of sin destroy from the human heart the natural repugnance to death and create even a purient desire to dwell among the victims of the last enemy."[1]

The Gadarene was a *disturbed* man and a disturber of men. The Word of God witnesses, "He cried out day and night." Dr. R. G. Lee lucidly and vividly penned of that poor soul:

> Those were cries that had in them the shriek of a man in the throes of a wild nightmare of a disordered brain or in the delirium of a devil-dominated heart and body. I think that in his bloodcurdling cry there was the coyote's howl, the tiger's snarl, the wolf's growl, the wild boar's grunt, the mad bull's bellow, the maniac's moan, the wounded eagle's scream, the whippoorwill's mournful wail, the hungry lion's roar, the plague carrying rat's squeak and shriek, and the horrible puff and breath of the death adder.[2]

And he was a *destructive* man, essentially a self-destroying sinner. Dominated by the Devil, body, mind and soul, he dishonored himself and sought to destroy himself, excising himself with stones or sharp objects across his face, down his arms, across his chest and belly, down his thighs and legs. Ghastly, gory, gruesome sight of a man. Gashed, lashed, smashed, flesh-bruised and bleeding, eyes glaring or staring in some hypnotic trance, groaning, moaning, cursing, crying, screaming, running, jumping, falling, groveling—the pathetic portrait of a sin-maddened, Satan-possessed sinner.

Then Jesus came!

Christ did not malign the man nor censure the sinner who fell at His feet, crying unto Him. In tenderest love, yet in severest command, He charged the demons to leave the victim. Well did Lee Scarborough state of our Savior:

Christ's authoritative word was backed by the power of a dominant love and this the demoniac evidently saw and recognized. This has ever been Christ's supreme instrument in breaking the shackles of sin. Jesus was never harsh nor cruel with plain, outspoken sinners, not even with this demoniac. He was harsh and used cutting words against hypocrites, those who feigned and cloaked themselves in robes of ecclesiastical or prideful righteousness, and had within their hearts "dead men's bones and uncleanness." But with out-and-out sinners Jesus showed every power of love as He did in this case.[3]

Christ converted, changed that maniac. One of Scripture's sweetest stories must be that conversion and its consequences. The demons were cast out, and immediately we see that saved sinner, "sitting, and clothed, and in his right mind" (Mark 5:15). No need of halfway houses for a halfway salvation! Christ's salvation is an instantaneous, mind-, heart-, will-transforming salvation (2 Cor. 5:17).

There was a change in body. His body was no longer the habitation of devils. There was a change in his mind. His spirit had been regenerated. Sitting! Not running around wildly. At the feet of Jesus. No longer an inhabitant of tombs! Clothed, no longer naked. Dressed, not denuded. Quiet, not quarrelsome. Calm, not crazy. The snarling mouth had been filled with praise. The clenched fist is now an open palm. The eyes of fury are now the eyes of faith. The heart that was the council chamber of devils is now a throne room of angels. The fierce fiend has become a gentle friend.[4]

Aye, in the words of the hymn writer:

"From home and friends the evil spirits drove him,
Among the tombs he dwelt in misery;
He cut himself as demon pow'rs possessed him,
Then Jesus came and set the captive free."

It needs to be added, what Christ did for him, He can do for you!

Christ not only converted that man. He commandeered him, commissioned him to be a co-laborer with Him in the field of evangelism!

The once crazed demoniac, who craved satyrs, the spirit world, immediately desired the fellowship and service of the Savior, praying Christ that he might accompany Him in His ministry. It takes no stretch of the imagination to sense the spiritual profit such a tour with Christ would produce in growth and grace in this new convert. Nor does it require any sweep of imagination to perceive what an asset such a convert would be on an evangelistic tour. He could be publicized as "from exorcism to evangelism," or, "former Satanist now preaches

90

Christ." All of which would have been proper and profitable! Surely the Savior shocked and temporarily saddened the new convert when He refused his offer and told him instead: "Go home to thy friends, and tell them how great things the Lord hath done for thee, and hath had compassion on thee" (Mark 5:19).

That had to be the most difficult field to serve Christ! When Christ had cast the demons from the demoniac, and they in subservience to the Savior obeyed, they asked His permission to inhabit something else, to which request Christ gave them liberty to inhabit hogs. The hogs then bolted, crashed into the sea and were choked. Irate citizens, rather than rejoicing in the deliverance of their tormented neighbor, rejected Christ, demanding He depart from their coasts. Instead of hallelujahs they harangued, preferring stinking swine to the Savior. This is the crowd to which Christ sent the converted demoniac to minister.

Hometown evangelism is difficult for many apparent reasons. A converted sinner's clean, holy life will be a constant rebuke to his sinning family and friends. But the lack of that clean, consecrated life will always be a greater detriment. If one's life does not match his lips, there is always the caustic rebuke: "You had better get yourself cleaned up before you try to convert me."

Admittedly, we often shy away from hometown evangelism of family and friends because of the fears of embarrassing loved ones, citing such statements as, "You know them so well. They will think you are preaching at them." Actually, the real problem usually is they know us too well! But the heart of the failure of reaching friends and family is not concern over feelings, but unconcern over the soul! Years ago in a revival meeting, the pastor wisely taught a soul-winning training course each evening before the meeting. One night he asked the question: "Why is it so hard to deal with our loved ones?" Many answers were stated. Suddenly one stood up and stated startlingly, "Pastor, the real reason is we don't care if they go to Hell or not!" I spoke out emphatically, "Amen!" That is the heart of the problem!

Hometown—family and friends—is the hardest area of evangelism. But it is one of the neediest areas. And it is also the first area of evangelism for the new convert.

There is Bible principle and precedent for that statement. The newly converted Andrew "first findeth his own brother . . . And he brought him [Peter] to Jesus" (John 1:41, 42). When Paul instructed the inquiring Philippian jailer how to be saved, he intoned: "Believe on the Lord Jesus Christ, and thou shalt be saved, and thy house" (Acts 16:31). Christ commissioned that newborn convert to "go home . . .

and tell them what great things the Lord hath done for thee. . . ."

Christ's job description to the converted Gadarene contains foundational facts for all who would obediently serve the Savior in evangelism to loved ones.

"Tell them *how great things* the Lord hath done for thee." Tell them your testimony, your personal experience. That is not a recital of what you believe about certain doctrines, creeds, confessions or churches, but that Christ saved you. And satisfies you. And succors you. And supplies your needs.

"Tell them how great things *the Lord* hath done for thee." That evangelism obligates one to tell *who* did the great things!

"Tell them how great things the Lord hath done for *thee.*" That commission obligates the convert to proclaim at home *why* he is witnessing! Because of gratitude to God for His great mercy! Because of the glory Christ should receive because of His goodness! Because of the great need of loved, lost family and friends for cleansing for their sin-stained souls; for contentment for their sin-sated souls; emancipation for their sin-shackled souls!

That converted demoniac sinner cleansed of his sins, delivered of his demons, charmed, conquered, commandeered by Christ obeyed his Lord. He "departed, and began to publish . . . how great things Jesus had done for him." And the Scriptures further relate, "and all men did marvel."

It is as one well witnessed, "Going home instead of going with Christ, he missed seeing Jesus open blind eyes, but he opened the eyes of others to the wonders Christ could do for them. He missed seeing Jesus make some deaf ears to hear, but he had the joy of knowing many ears heard the wonder and the works of Christ."

I wonder out loud: How many converts to Christ will there be in Heaven who came from the streets, shops, shores, fields and farms of Decapolis and Gadarene country because a converted maniac went home and told his family and his friends that Jesus came and had compassion on him and did great things for him!

NOTES:

1. W. B. Riley, *Bible of the Expositor and Evangelist's New Testament* (Cleveland: Union Gospel Press, 1926), 2:34.

2. R. G. Lee, *Bread from Bellevue Oven* (Murfreesboro, TN: Sword of the Lord Publishers, 1947), p. 107.

3. Lee R. Scarborough, *How Jesus Won Men* (Nashville: Sunday School Board of the Southern Baptist Convention, 1926), p. 101.

4. Lee, *Bread from Bellevue Oven,* p. 119.

Good Samaritan

Christ's Kind of Christian

Luke 10:37 has to be one of the most spectacular sentences Christ ever spoke. He never said anything similar to it in His earthly ministry. In that one instance Christ singled out a mortal man and cited him as the example to all Christians evermore in their service for Christ.

All other times He challenged Christians to imitate Himself in their walk and work: "Follow me, and I will make you fishers of men"; "For I have given you an example, that ye should do as I have done to you"; "As my Father hath sent me, even so send I you."

But on one occasion, Christ cited a Samaritan traveler on the Jericho Road and made him His personal, prime example of evangelism by charging: "Go, and do thou likewise." The study of that Samaritan immediately becomes a study of contrasts of men and motives, conflicts of emotions, all compounded in the crucible of a sermon by the Lord Jesus.

The setting is a torturous, twisting, steep, strong, robber-infested road that originated at the northwest gate of Jerusalem, 2,500 feet above sea level, and terminated in the subtropical city of Jericho, verdant with palms, pomegranates and citrus, 900 feet below sea level. The road is the storied Jericho Road of sermon and song. Josephus, Jewish historian of the first century, judged it, however, as the "Bloody Way." In its wilderness areas robbers lay in wait in stony cliffs, surveying sweeping sections of the road from the camouflaged hiding haunts. Then they sprang upon unsuspecting travelers, wounding or killing their victims, robbing them of their possessions, then retreating back to their haunts to await another strike.

Such an incident occasioned Christ's sermon in Luke 10:30-37. Immediately He introduced five individuals. First, the traveler, waylaid and robbed, wounded and abandoned to die. Second, in a quick sweep, Christ introduces two religious men, a priest and a Levite, traveling individually, men who came upon the waylaid victim but passed by on the other side. Third, an innkeeper is seen in a single sentence, somewhat incidental to the drama on the road. Then the Savior sketches the Samaritan.

He is seen in dramatic contrast with the two religious leaders, whom I have described as Criminal Christians, men blind-eyed, deaf-eared, lame-legged to a man in his need because they were scaredy-cat-hearted and selfish-souled servants of God. In contrast to these "Criminal Christians," R. G. Lee wrote of the Samaritan:

> The two had twice the eyes but not half the spiritual discernment of the good Samaritan. The two lived twice the time, but the good Samaritan lived the most. The two outnumbered the good Samaritan two to one, but he outweighed them both. The two traveled the fastest, but the good Samaritan traveled the best![1]

The reason for Lee's rationale is most obvious—the Samaritan went to and ministered to the highway victim. And that Samaritan visitation and ministration is immortalized in the pages of sacred history and occasioned Christ to picture him as the portrait of His kind of Christian worker!

The Samaritan had *lifted up eyes*—a vision of helpless, hopeless humanity on the highways. Christ said of him, "He saw him." That spells spiritual sight! It is the same look on the lost, the least, the last the Lord Jesus had! Christ epitomized His own evangelistic ministry in this succinct sentence: "For the Son of man is come to *seek* and to save that which was lost" (Luke 19:10). And he did. Only a sampling of Scripture instances must suffice: "But when he *saw* the multitudes, he was moved with compassion"; "And Jesus went forth, and *saw* a great multitude"; "And as Jesus passed forth from thence, he *saw* a man, named Matthew"; "And Jesus, when he came out [of the ship], *saw* much people, and was moved with compassion toward them"; "Now as he walked by the sea of Galilee, he *saw* Simon and Andrew his brother."

The Samaritan walked with his eyes lifted, looking, even as Christ had commanded His disciples at a Samaritan well one noon hour: "Lift up your eyes, and look on the fields; for they are white already to harvest." His daily prayer, His daily purpose may well be that petition of Betty Stam as she sobbed:

> Open my eyes, that I may see
> This one and that one needing Thee:
> Hearts that are dumb, unsatisfied;
> Lives that are dark, for whom Christ died.
>
> Open my eyes in sympathy
> Clear into man's deep soul to see;
> Wise with Thy wisdom to discern,
> And with Thy heart of love to yearn.
>
> Open my eyes in power, I pray,
> Give me the strength to speak today,
> Someone to bring, dear Lord, to Thee;
> Use me, O Lord, use even me.

The Samaritan had a *lifted up heart of compassion,* for Christ commented: "And when he saw him, he had compassion on him." Compassion is a word of Latin derivation, meaning "to suffer with." Thus our Savior suggested of the Samaritan that when he saw that mangled man—with his every muscle torn, twisted, throbbing in pain, his flesh on fire with fever, his mind moved, maddened in delirium—that Samaritan's heart hungered that he might take every ache, every break, every suffering, every sorrow into his own breast. Beloved, that is compassion! And that Scripture further suggests that when the Samaritan saw the man lying there alone, health lost, wealth lost, life disgorging with every drop of blood, he would have taken all that loneliness and lostness into his own soul. Aye, that is compassion!

Surely we must see his similarity to the Savior of whom the Word witnesses: "But when he saw the multitudes, he was moved with compassion on them, because they fainted, and were scattered abroad, as sheep having no shepherd"; "And Jesus went forth, and saw a great multitude, and was moved with compassion toward them, and healed their sick"; "I have compassion on the multitude, because they . . . have nothing to eat"; "So Jesus had compassion on them [two blind men], and touched their eyes"; "And Jesus, moved with compassion . . . touched him, and saith unto him . . . be thou clean"; "The Lord . . . hath had compassion on thee [a crazed, demon possessed man in the tombs]"; "When the Lord saw her [a widowed mother whose only son had died], he had compassion on her."

I have stated seven instances of Christ's compassion, a compassion mirrored by the Samaritan, but a compassion no man could fully mirror. Christ's compassion was the compassion of God that would not only weep over the lost, warn the lost, and woo the lost to Himself, but would finally compel Him to pour out His soul as the Sacrifice of Calvary's cross to win the lost!

But be sure the Samaritan had:

> ". . . A heart that is burdened
> Infused with a passion to pray;
> . . . A heart like my Savior,
> Who, being in agony prayed;
> Such caring for others, Lord, give me
> On my heart let the burden be laid."

The *Samaritan had lifted up feet of visitation.* The Savior spoke of him, "And [he] went to him." Going, calling, seeking, visiting—that is good Samaritan service—Christ's kind of Christianity!

The Samaritan could have performed spiritual services "afar off." If it were today, he could have purchased a lace-lined, embossed, Scripture-reference, Annie-Johnson-Flint-rhymed get well card or even some fragrant flowers and had them delivered to that gore-soaked, pain-racked wretch on the Jericho Road. He could have also prayed, and this is no depreciation of the priority place and power and pressing need of prayer! But the Samaritan knew that dying soul needed more than a friend with folded hands in petition to Heaven for healing. He needed hands lifted up to hold his head; hands lifted to compassionately wash away the gore and grime and soothe his fevered face; hands lifted to place refreshing liquid to his parched, pained lips; hands lifted to stanch the flow of life-draining blood, fashion splints and bind broken limbs; and hands lifted to carry him to a nearby hostel where there was rest and security. Aye, he needed a visit! A call! A friend to come and minister!

In that single errand of mercy, the Samaritan showed what was close to the heart of Christ. We read of our Savior's pulsing, passionate ministry of three years of fervent, feverish evangelism compressed into

96

one sentence: "And Jesus *went* about all the cities and villages, teaching . . . and preaching . . . and healing."

The consummate virtue of all was the Samaritan's *lifted up soul of dedication.* He was sold out! That spells out the Samaritan's heart and soul. Sold out! That is the real reason he saw that bloody, butchered man on that lonely, forsaken highway. Sold out! That is the real reason he heard the convulsing, crying call of a dying man on that foreboding Jericho Road. Sold out! That is why he had compassion on that helpless, hemorrhaging highway victim. Sold out! That is why he ran to his rescue. Sold out! That is why he, unlike the Levite and priest, did not look aghast, appalled at that writhing, wailing victim of robbers, then look apprehensively at the rocky cliffs fearful that the same robbers might return to slay him if he stopped to save the life of the unfortunate sufferer. No! He was sold out! He would risk life and limb to minister to a man because his time, his talents, his treasure, his life, body, brain and blood were no longer his. They belonged to another!

It is only speculation on my part, but in my mind I muse, Did that Samaritan—a man of a despised, half-breed race, as well as a fallen sinner of Adam's race—prior to that Jericho Road journey, did he hear Christ preach on some other highway, in some thronging crowd in the Temple, marketplace, mountainside, seashore, or even at Sychar in Samaria? And I wonder, Did he face up to his sins, forsake them, confess them, calling upon Christ for forgiveness then sell out to the Savior, crowning Him Lord of his newly begotten life?

Careful consideration of the man causes me to think it is more than musing of the mind. He was constrained by a compelling compassion. Such is the gift of God (Rom. 5:5). He was controlled by an unflinching courage. Such is a mark of a Holy Spirit controlled Christian (Acts 13:9, 10). He was thoroughly consecrated. He gave all of himself to the man in need on the Jericho Road. Then he carried him on his beast to an inn where he could have shelter, protection, provision and attention. Then on the morrow, he enlisted the innkeeper to continue ministering to him until his complete recovery, concluding his appeal with the selfless spirit of Christ, "Whatsoever thou spendest more, when I come again, I will repay thee." His was love without calculation. He served without counting the cost. It was this kind of compassion, courage, commitment and consecration that prompted Christ to cite the Samaritan as His human example of Christian service.

NOTE:

1. R. G. Lee, *From Feet to Fathoms* (Grand Rapids: Zondervan Publishing House, 1926), p. 26.

James

Mr. Camel Knees Christian

My title is not altogether original since as far back as the second century we have the record of Hegesippus, who wrote of James, the half brother of Christ, "He was in the habit of entering into the temple alone, and was often found upon his bended knees, asking for forgiveness of the people; so that his knees became hard like a camel's knees in consequence of his habitual supplication and kneeling before God."[1]

A Christian wholly sold out to prayer. That one fact alone makes James worthy of inclusion in the registry of these Bible worthies, witnesses God has singled out in the Scriptures to challenge us in our ministries, our motivations, our masteries.

But James was a most remarkable man in many other respects. James was kin to Christ in that special sense that only a handful can ever claim. He was blood related, a half brother to Christ, a son of Joseph and Mary. Any other interpretation of Galatians 1:19 ("But other of the apostles saw I none, save James the Lord's brother") is actually an argument for the perpetual virginity of Mary, and makes a mystical, spiritual relationship between Christ and James rather than the literal, physical affiliation.

As a brother to Christ, James had to be aware and awed by his older brother. Since Scripture is so silent about the Lord's first thirty years, alluding only to His mental, physical, spiritual and social growth as a youth (Luke 2:52) and His Temple experiences when He was an eight-day-old babe and then His interrogating and instructing the Temple theologians when He was twelve, all else stated about our Savior must border somewhat on supposition.

Yet it is for sure that James had to witness Christ's daily, undefiled life, hear His sanctified speech—words weighted with wisdom and seasoned with salt—and observe Christ's faithfulness to the synagogue and the spiritual affairs of life. After Christ's baptism in the Jordan River by John the Baptist, James and all the family of Joseph had to be mightily aware of Christ's meteoric ministry. It is for sure he heard about, if he did not witness, some of Christ's mighty miracles, explainable only by supernatural power. He, on occasion, had to hear or hear about Christ's unprecedented preaching: the sublime, sacred truths of the Sermon on the Mount; the prolific, princely, practical parables; the apocalyptic anathemas thundered against religious racketeers, and always, messages of mercy, exhorting repentance and inviting the penitent, promises of peace and pardon.

These mighty ministries James knew personally, as well as that awful week—now called Holy Week—in which Christ rode into Jerusalem as Israel's king, quickly to be hounded and harassed by the unbelieving, rejecting religious leaders; eventually to be betrayed into their murderous hands, illegally tried and sentenced to death; finally to be crucified on Calvary's cross. James was no stranger to all this.

James totally rejected Christ's Messiahship to Israel and His Sonship with the Father which He proclaimed and proved to many who believed on Him. Some scholars suggest that James' legalistic Jewish mind and his pharisaical allegiance to the Law of Moses and the traditions were "insulted by Christ's absolute freedom from all such unscriptural trammels."

But one blessed day James believed in His elder brother, accepted Him as his Messiah, crowned Him Lord of his life, received

Him as Savior for his sinful soul. On that day James saw his brother not just as Mary's son but as the *resurrected* Son of God! Paul penned of that epochal, eventful experience, "After that, he [Christ] was seen of James" (1 Cor. 15:7).

That revelation of the resurrected Christ transformed James. He became a believer, but more than that, a fervent follower, a devoted disciple, a consecrated churchman, a spiritual saint, a powerful penman and a pattern of prayer!

Immediately after his conversion, we see James associated with the believers in the early church. Soon we witness him in a place of authority in that apostolic company, helping settle doctrinal disputes (Acts 15:1-34). In that particular instance, James was chairman of the council called into question over a raging controversy, "Except ye [Gentile converts to Christ] be circumcised after the manner of Moses, ye cannot be saved." James' adjudgment has rightfully been called the "Believer's Emancipation Proclamation." Citing Simon Peter's revelation and experience from God, and calling upon the authority of revealed Scriptures, James' judgment was: "That we trouble not them, which from among the Gentiles are turned to God." The ascetic, legalistic James proclaimed fundamental Bible truth that day: salvation by grace alone!

Later we find James to be one of the Holy Spirit-inspired penmen of the pages of Scripture, writing an epistle of comfort, correction and counsel to Christians in their great practical, spiritual responsibilities.

James' epistle has been likened to the Book of Proverbs in the Old Testament since it deals with the "practical application of truth in everyday situations, setting forth these ethical requirements in vivid, homely language." Curtis Vaughn wrote:

> That which distinguishes James most of all, however, is not its likeness to the wisdom literature [of the Old Testament] but its remarkable similarity to the words of Jesus. Indeed James exhibits greater likeness to the teachings of Jesus than any other book in the New Testament. . . . A recent study lists twenty-six allusions to his words. . . . Every page of James gives evidence of the influence of Jesus. . . . James, in its tone, is probably the most authoritative of all the New Testament epistles. In the 108 verses of the letter there are 54 imperative verbs.[2]

Read its pages. Be charged, changed, charmed by its precepts. Space prohibits even merest mention of all its practical contents. I trust you don't weary of the word *practical*. That is what the Book of James is: practical preaching by a practical preacher who had seen the pure, practical Christian life lived to perfection by his brother Jesus Christ for three decades.

100

I am quick to add that James practiced what he preached. His was no "Do as I say, but don't do as I do" pedagogy. His piety of life earned him another nickname: "James the Just." Quoting again from Hegesippus who wrote of James' Nazarite nature: "He drank neither wine nor strong drink, and abstained from animal food. A razor never came upon his head; he never anointed himself with oil. . . . He never wore woollen, but only fine linen garments."[3] It is most evident from several Scriptures that James gave strict adherence to the Law (Acts 21:17-26; Gal. 2:12). In this he is charged by some commentators as being a legalist and a Pharisee. Regardless, James' exhortations to holy living—inspired by the Holy Spirit—are a constant challenge and a real rebuke to all of us, too often!

Doubtlessly, James' injunctions to a consistent, persistent prayer life are one of his most serious censures of twentieth-century Christians. The vital place of prayer permeates the pages of his little letter:

> . . . Ask of God, that giveth to all men liberally, and upbraideth not; and it shall be given him (1:5).
>
> Ye have not, because ye ask not. Ye ask, and receive not, because ye ask amiss, that ye may consume it upon your lusts (4:2, 3).
>
> Is any among you afflicted? let him pray. Is any merry? let him sing psalms. Is any sick among you? let him call for the elders of the church; and let them pray over him, anointing him with oil in the name of the Lord: And the prayer of faith shall save the sick, and the Lord shall raise him up; and if he have committed sins, they shall be forgiven him (5:13-15).
>
> Confess your faults one to another, and pray one for another, that ye may be healed. The effectual fervent prayer of a righteous man availeth much (5:16).
>
> Elias [Elijah] was a man subject to like passions as we are, and he prayed earnestly that it might not rain: and it rained not on the earth by the space of three years and six months. And he prayed again, and the heaven gave rain, and the earth brought forth her fruit (5:17, 18).

These are instructions from a man who practiced prayer and profited through prayer. What an impeachment Mr. Camel Knees is to our anemic, apathetic, spasmodic, powerless, fruitless twentieth-century Christianity which has substituted pep for power, enthusiasm for anointing, supper rooms for upper rooms, saying prayers instead of interceding in prayer, talking about prayer instead of travailing in prayer. May James, the apostle of prayer, challenge us to cry unto Christ, even as the disciples did back yonder, "Lord, teach us to pray!"

Alexander Whyte wrote of James, ". . . He was such a man of

prayer that when they came to coffin him his knees were as hard and stiff as the knees of a camel."[4] Aye, meet Mr. Camel Knees in these paragraphs and tonight, as you prepare for bed, meet yourself by taking a long, critical look at your knees and at your prayer life!

NOTES:

1. J. Sidlow Baxter, *Explore the Book*, 6 vols. (Grand Rapids: Zondervan Publishing House, 1960), 6:285.
2. Curtis Vaughn, *A Study Guide: James* (Grand Rapids: Zondervan Publishing House, 1969), pp. 8, 9.
3. Baxter, *Explore the Book*, 6:285.
4. Whyte, *Whyte's Bible Characters*, p. 144.

John
(Apostle)

Penman Preacher

No treatment of New Testament evangelism would be true or complete without a study of the apostle John. And this statement is totally true despite the absolutely amazing fact that there is not one single Scripture account of any sermon John ever spoke, any revival campaign he ever conducted, no, not even one convert that he ever claimed for Christ.

Yet in light of the fact that John was one of Christ's closest, choicest companions and a vital leader of the apostles; and in light of the fire and force of the evangelistic emphasis that pulsingly permeates the pages of his writings, it is not simply sentimental supposition to state that John surely preached soul-winning sermons and successfully practiced personal evangelism. No, it is a most plausible possibility to pen that John was a successful winner of souls for the Savior!

However, it is in his powerful and peerless penmanship, and not in his preaching and personal work, for which the world will be forever indebted to John. Well did Lee Scarborough write in an article, "John—Soul-winning Journalist" (pages that were profitable to my ministry years ago, and that prompted me to pen this particular profile):

> John's evangelistic contribution to Christ's kingdom was in the line of evangelistic journalism. John was the soul-winning journalist. He was the greatest spiritual interpreter of the inner life of Jesus Christ . . . and he made a faithful record of much that Christ said and much that He did.[1]

Limited lines prohibit any exhaustive survey of the evangelistic emphasis in the journals of John, but may I make mention of a few of the most famous examples of evangelism as pictured by the penman preacher? See them. Study them. Seek to imitate them. May they shame us, startle us, speak to us, shake us out of our laziness and lethargy. May they melt, mold, move us to earnest, ever-pleading, ever-persisting personal evangelism. May they call, charge, compel, constrain us to follow our living, loving Lord and those New Testament soul-winning worthies in their shining trail of evangelism.

(1) John's journal recorded one of Jesus' first converts—a Jewish youth named Andrew. Charmed by Christ, then converted and conquered by Him, Andrew was constrained to first go and find his own brother, Peter, and bring him to Jesus. This is family evangelism—personal evangelism in its highest, holiest hour (John 1:40-42).

(2) John is the writer who left us the immortal record of Christ's conversation with Nicodemus. This was evangelism with the up-and-out, religious-but-lost sinner (John 3:1-21).

(3) Only John told us the thrilling tale of Christ converting the shameful, scarlet-stained, sin-scarred Samaritan woman at the well. This was evangelism at the down-and-out level (John 4:1-30).

(4) John gave the only record of Christ's campaign at Sychar, a two-day "foreign missionary" evangelistic effort among the hated and heathen Samaritans (John 4:34-43).

(5) John alone recorded Christ's converting the harlot who was caught in the act of her sordid sin—evangelism of the out-and-out sinner (John 8:1-11).

104

(6) And John recounted the blessed story of the Savior restoring the sight and redeeming the soul of the blind man—evangelism that ministers to the physical needs to open the door of ministry to the spiritual needs of sinners (John 9:1-34).

John's journals record some of Heaven's greatest evangelistic promises—promises penned to meet sinful man's deepest poverties. They will ever be considered among the chiefest, choicest declarations of God's limitless love for the lost and His most passionate pleas and promises for sinners' salvation seen in the Scriptures. These are passages for us to pray over; print and propagate by tracts, booklets, books, Sunday school literature everywhere and all the time; passages to preach and plead with sinners to get saved. See a few among the multiplied many from John's pen: John 1:11, 12; John 3:16; John 5:24; John 6:37; John 10:9; 1 John 1:9; Revelation 3:20.

Only merest mention can be made of John's journal that records some of the most consummate, compelling commands to Christians to evangelize a lost world for the Savior. What saint can ignore them without committing greatest, grossest iniquity, insubordination and infamy:

(1) John 4:35—the challenge of unharvested harvest fields.
(2) John 15:16—Christ's charge, call and command to all Christians.
(3) John 20:21—compulsion to evangelize by Christ's example.
(4) John 21:15-18—the constraint because of love for the Lord.

May God be pleased to raise up in our ranks a host of writers who will help witness to a lost world by penning and propagating God's gospel—the "good news"—through the printed page!

NOTE:

1. Lee R. Scarborough, *Endued To Win* (Nashville: Sunday School Board of the Southern Baptist Convention, 1922), p. 244.

John Mark

Christian Worker Who Came Back

To be praised in print as "profitable to me" by the apostle Paul would be the paragon of praise, indeed. Yet those are the exact words the aged apostle penned about John Mark to Timothy shortly before Paul was to become a martyr for his Lord. "Take Mark, and bring him with thee: for he is profitable to me for the ministry" (2 Tim. 4:11), Paul penned in his letter preserved for us by the Holy Spirit.

Mark did not always hold that place of esteem in the eyes of the elder evangelist. In fact, on Paul's first missionary journey Mark was the source of a contention that caused schism and a split between Paul and Barnabas, a rift that never was rectified as far as Bible record reveals.

Acts 12:25—13:13 describes the origin of that first missionary journey, organized for the cause of evangelism for Christ. The first missionary party was commissioned by the church at Jerusalem to sail from Antioch to preach Christ to people who had never heard His saving Name. The verses are electric with the spine-tingling early exploits and possibilities of that evangelism. The names of that select, elect group of evangelists and soul-winning worthies entrusted with evangelizing the unreached, the unsaved, the untouched of Asia Minor were Paul, Barnabas and his nephew, John Mark.

But that evangelistic endeavor was soon crippled. In one of the saddest sentences of Scripture we read, "Now when Paul and his company loosed from Paphos, they came to Perga in Pamphylia: and John departing from them returned to Jerusalem" (Acts 13:13). Many reasons have been suggested for Mark becoming the first missionary turncoat who would leave the conquests of whitened harvest fields of perishing heathen to return to the comforts of home and the caresses of loved ones.

Scripture gives no specifics, but doubtlessly Alexander Maclaren discovered and described as well as any the heart of Mark's defection when he wrote:

> It was not a departure from Christ, but it was a departure from very plain duty. And if you will notice the point of time at which Mark threw up the work that was laid upon him, you will see the reason for his doing so. The first place to which the bold evangelists went was Cyprus. Barnabas was a native of Cyprus, which was perhaps the reason for selecting it as the place in which to begin the mission. For the same reason, because it was the native place of his relative, it would be very easy work for John Mark as long as they stopped in Cyprus, among his friends, with people that knew him, and with whom no doubt he was familiar. But as soon as they crossed the strait that separated the island from the mainland, and set foot upon the soil of Asia Minor, so soon he turned tail; like some recuit, that goes into battle, full of fervour, but as soon as the bullets began to "ping" makes the best of his way to the rear.[1]

Another major factor that may well have militated against Mark serving his Savior in missionary ministry was his early association with ease of environment. Mark was the son of a well-to-do woman, Acts 12:12-14 would suggest. As such he could have been sheltered and coddled by a doting parent. Thus when Mark left Cyprus, his friends and his family for Pamphylia and the high mountain ranges of Asia Minor that predicated privation, poverty, discomforts, possible disease and death, it is easy to see why he could decide to go home to the comforts, the calm, the companionship of a mother, to money and to the other material conveniences of life.

But something happened to John Mark between the sad and shameful sentence of Acts 13:13 and the tender, touching testimonial of the apostle Paul regarding Mark and his profitableness as recorded in 2 Timothy 4:11. The Scriptures shed not one suggestion as to what transpired—but it is no assumption nor supposition to say that John Mark got right with his Lord and with Paul. And there were blessed results of Mark's restoration and revival. He became again the trusted traveling companion of the apostle Paul—and probably Peter, his spiritual father (1 Pet. 5:13). But Mark realized his highest and most honored-of-God usefulness for Christ when he was chosen by Christ to be the penman of the second Gospel portraying the life of our Lord. Well did Harry Ironside comment on Mark: "It is like God to select the one-time unfaithful servant Mark to tell the story of the ever-faithful Servant—His own blessed Son!" Amen!

As I mention Mark—his failures, his fumblings, his fall; but also his restoration, his revival and rise again to a place of purpose and profit, aye, even praise, in his service for his Lord—I am quick to make mention that the same grace of God that pardoned and restored Mark to his place of usefulness is still present and plenteous today for any stumbling, sinning saint who will return to the Lord, repent of his sin and receive that gift of God's great grace.

NOTE:

1. Alexander Maclaren, *Expositions of Holy Scripture: The Acts* (New York: Hodder & Stoughton, n.d.), 2:18, 19.

John the Baptist

Unprecedented Preacher

No study of Heaven's heroes would be complete, or even correct, that did not include in a preeminent place the person of John the Baptist. For this cousin of Christ's—a man of the mountains, clad in camel-hair clothing and living on simple fare of locusts and wild honey—was the inaugural evangelist. There had been prophets before him, preachers before him; but John the Baptist introduced and initiated a new ministry from God to mankind: a gospel-preaching evangelism! He had no predecessors, but as another has wonderfully written, "Thank God, he has had multiplied thousands of glorious successors."

John the Baptist was not only the inaugural evangelist; he is in every area of manhood and ministry the ideal evangelist. Any evangelist who is seeking the praises and the plaudits of Christ Who called him into the vital field of evangelism must study and simulate the ministry, the make-up, the methods, yea, the matchless motives of this country preacher. Christ never pronounced higher eulogies of a man than He did of John the Baptist. "Yea, I say unto you, and [he was] more than a prophet" (Matt. 11:9), said the Savior, "thus placing John above that galaxy of worthies, which constituted the chief glory of the Hebrew nation." But Christ said more than this. He declared that "among them that are born of women there hath not risen a greater than John the Baptist" (Matt. 11:11), thus lifting him to the loftiest pinnacle of human praise!

In limited lines of space may I list some of the essential elements that characterized this earliest evangelist who still stands out after nearly twenty centuries as one of the greatest soul-winning worthies this world has ever known? May God grant us grace to initiate and imitate him in these desperate, dangerous and deteriorating days of this twentieth century is my prayer.

(1) His ministry was marked by a deathless devotion to proclaim Christ. "And I saw, and bare record that this is the Son of God" (John 1:34). "Behold the Lamb of God, which taketh away the sin of the world" (John 1:29) was the unchanging, unwavering theme of John's preaching. Nothing could alter the message of this man sent from God to introduce Heaven's Son and the world's Savior. Neither passions, pride, pursuit for power, the praise of men, promotion and place, preservation of life, popularity, personal gain—no! nothing could seduce John the Baptist from pursuing the supreme passion of his life: proclaiming the Person of Jesus Christ.

(2) John's ministry was marked by an emphasis on the God-given essentials of the evangelistic message. Powerfully, passionately, pungently he preached on truths that had long since been forgotten and forsaken: repentance, righteousness, regeneration, remission of sins. John was a Voice—a voice that in thundering tones pointed out the sham, the shallowness of hypocritical hearts and ritualistic religion. John was a Voice—a voice that in terrible tones preached against sin. Relentlessly, ruthlessly, probingly, personally, pointedly, John assailed sin: death-dealing, Hell-deserving, soul-damning, sure-retribution sin; whether in high places, in kings' palaces, or in low places of peasants' pastures. John was a Voice—a voice that in tenderest tones pleaded

110

with sin-laden and sin-sated sinners to repent. His was a clarion voice calling for a "genuine, soul-converting, heart-cleansing, life-purifying repentance, carrying with it fruit in life and conduct."[1]

(3) John's ministry was marked by an enthronement of and an enduement by the Holy Ghost of God that kindled in his sin-abhorring, Spirit-of-God-ablaze soul an inextinguishable passion, an indomitable purpose, and an irresistible power and persuasion that ignited revival fires across the length and breadth of the country, from the commoners' cottages to the kings' courts; and influenced multitudes, publicans, Pharisees, priests, scribes, Sadducees, soldiers, yea, sinners of all sorts, to repentance and reception of the Kingdom of Heaven. Small wonder Christ summarized John's sweeping, transforming, conquering ministry: "He was a burning and a shining light" (John 5:35).

Scarcity of space prohibits further sentences that point out the shining spiritual essentials that stirred and spurred this great soul to earnest and effective evangelism, but may I pen a concluding paragraph by Lee R. Scarborough. May it speak to your heart as it has to mine:

> A life wholly given to God in soul-winning in the hills of Judaea in a remote age has cast a golden glory and given a radiant hope to all subsequent history. Jesus said that John, the simple, country, Baptist preacher, was the greatest born of women. By God's assize, a country preacher leads humanity's greatness. He introduced the Saviour to a ruined world and pointed men to Him. The first man among men, thank God, is the soul winner. Introduce the same Saviour, point sinners to Him, preach the same gospel in the power of the divine Spirit, and you will walk the way of Divine favor and glory.[2]

NOTES:

1. Lee R. Scarborough, *With Christ After the Lost* (Nashville: Sunday School Board of the Southern Baptist Convention, 1919), p. 62.
2. Ibid.

Judas Iscariot

Defecting Disciple

This chronicle would not be complete without the sad, shocking study of the evil evangelist, Judas Iscariot, of whom the Scriptures speak in bitterest and blighting epitaph: "He [went] to his own place" (Acts 1:25).

Some readers may recoil, rebutting that Judas should never be included in the royal register of Heaven's worthies. I agree that he is not entitled to inclusion in that select company except as he is shown to be in the Scriptures, the warning example of the errors and evils that workers for God must avoid and avert.

Judas' epitaph is written in Heaven's register as "deceiver," "devil," "hypocrite," "son of perdition," "suicide," "traitor." But few, if any, Christian workers ever had more privileges and possibilities to be a success in their service than did Judas. This native of Kerioth was personally selected by Christ to become one of that company of twelve chosen men called the apostles—men of such mien as Simon Peter, John, James, Andrew among others. As such, he was ordained of Christ to preach, win the lost, heal the sick, raise the dead, cast out devils (Matt. 10:5-8).

Moreover, Judas lived in most intimate contact with Christ for three years. He heard the Savior preach. He heard Him pray. He witnessed the might, the miracles in the ministry of the Master. And Judas enjoyed some of the most intimate relationships with Christ. He walked and talked with Him along many a mile on lonely, dusty trails. He witnessed Him weep over sinners, even that apostolic group. He was present when Christ "forgave the harlots, received the outcasts, gave hope to the hopeless, preached the Gospel to the needy." He supped at the same table with Christ, said his prayers in the presence of Christ, shared and slept in the same rooms with Christ, spent three whole years of his life with the Lord. Only eleven other men in human history had those same privileges!

Judas also seemingly met all the standards that would insure success in soul-winning service. He outwardly passed every test for apostleship. He appeared to be a firm believer in faith in Christ. He was obedient to believer's baptism. He was honored by the eleven, who elected him to be their treasurer, signifying his integrity, honesty, a life above reproach. Judas seemingly possessed every spiritual gift of the other apostles: preaching, performing miracles, praying, personal witnessing. Added to that array of evidence of Christian gifts, Judas exhibited great Christian grace. There are no recorded displays of the marks of carnality seen so often in the other disciples: the temper tantrums of Peter and John; the jealous, covetous spirit of James and John; the failure of faith of Peter.

In fact, Judas so exemplified the credentials and characteristics of spirituality that he was never suspect that he was not heart and soul, mind and spirit, one of the twelve. In Christ's numerous and various accusations that in that group there was a fifth columnist, a devil, a betrayer, a deceiver—not one of the other eleven suspected Judas.

But he was that man and eventually, at the opportune time, Judas became a turncoat against the truth personified in Christ, rejected Him who would be his redeemer, bargained with the enemy and betrayed Christ in the Garden of Gethsemane, thus selling his soul to Hell for a mere thirty pieces of silver.

That is a capsule commentary on the man, but Judas' biography is not complete without a study of the psychiatry of the man. A study of the Scriptures reveals the secret sin of Judas' soul. As Harry Ironside intoned, "There was one sin that controlled his inmost being, and in large measure dictated his behavior, and that was the sin of covetousness." Doubtlessly when Judas joined the apostolic company he was not cursed with a greed for gold. But somewhere, sometime, that lust was conceived. Despite the many, yes, multiplied messages and warning words our Savior spoke about the greed for gold and the ruinous result of riches, Judas fed and fired his soul with the greed of making gain in his office. His calm, composed, seemingly Christian exterior hid that sordid secret: preeminence, wealth, power in the kingdom of Christ.

For a season Judas could and would suffer inpoverishments, frugal food, sleeping in fields, misunderstanding and malignment of the Pharisees and the political leaders. In Christ's miracles, popularity and power he envisioned a great worldwide king and twelve rulers—and he was one of them! But one day that bauble began to burst. John 6 records that Christ's sharp, spiritual sermons started preaching the crowds away. Day by day His popularity waned and finally waxed into persecution. Judas' dream had turned into a nightmare.

Judas then sensed that time was short to satisfy his greed for gold. He decided on a desperate, diabolical, damnable plot: he would betray Christ to the Pharisees for the best price he could command. His opportunity came. It was Passover time. Emotions of the people were at fever pitch. Christ walked and worked at night because the inflamed Jews were seeking to slay Him. He and His disciples were going to the Garden of Gethsemane. Judas secured the schedule, then impiously petitioned the priests, "What will you give me if I deliver him into your hands?" They covenanted for thirty pieces of silver, the price of a slave. We shudder at such blatant, blasphemous, blackness-of-night bargain. But I am quick to cite, some reader may be selling his soul for even less—a bottle of booze, a deck of cards, a joint of drugs, the lust of the flesh, the pride of life, ignoring as did Judas the Savior's eternally wise warning, "What shall it profit a man, if he shall gain the whole world, and lose his own soul?"

Later that night, after supper—Judas' last opportunity to repent—Judas rushed from the meal and his Master's rebuking words, "One of you shall betray me," recruited the enemy, returned with them to the Garden and then in ruinous, defecting kiss revealed Christ to the enemy in his rejection of Him.

114

Hours later, a remorseful but nonrepentant Judas, condemned by his conscience, returned to the priests to cast that galling, haunting thirty pieces of silver at their feet. Then in the blackest, bitterest hour of crisis in his life, no one to turn to, no way to turn, Judas crashed out into the blackness of his night to commit suicide and, as the Bible bitterly relates, "by transgression fell, that he might go to his own place" (Acts 1:25).

Judas Iscariot is surely seen in the Scriptures as a warning light to every servant of the Savior; first, to insure, assure himself that he is genuinely converted to Christ and not merely a mouthpiece of the gospel, knowing only the language but not knowing the Lord (Matt. 7:21-23); a mere professor but not a possessor of salvation; simply a carnal, respectable, but unsaved sinner like Judas who "fell out of the brightest light, out of the tenderest companionship and fellowship of Jesus—the best of men; of Christ, the Holy Son of God; and headlong with his unredeemed, sinful soul plunged into the deepest punishment of the blackest Hell."[1]

Judas Iscariot, secondly, is Christ's warning example to all who engage in evangelism to beware, be on guard, avoid, abstain from every appearance, every association, every suggestion of evil. Avoid what Lee Scarborough stated was the "money heart": "That greed-loving covetousness that has strewn the road to Christian power with the wreck of the money heart."[2] And not only the "money heart," but the "maiden heart," and the "most-successful-ministry heart," the "majoring-on-minors heart," and the many other means that the Devil dangles before men, to deceive, deter, dull, deaden, destroy men's ministries.

In the light of the lessons learned from Judas, every Christian worker would be wise to read, and read often, the warnings of Peter and Paul (warnings which in no wise assault the blessed truth of the security of the believer in the Savior) to men and their ministries: "Wherefore the rather, brethren, give diligence to make your calling and election sure: for if ye do these things, ye shall never fall" (2 Pet. 1:10); and, "Take heed unto thyself, and unto the doctrine; continue in them: for in doing this thou shalt both save thyself, and them that hear thee" (1 Tim. 4:16).

NOTES:

1. Scarborough, *Endued To Win*, p. 261.
2. Ibid., p. 260.

Matthew
From Disgrace to Discipleship

"And as Jesus passed forth from thence, he saw a man, named Matthew, sitting at the receipt of custom: and he saith unto him, Follow me. And he arose, and followed him" (Matt. 9:9). "That was Matthew's modest way of telling all generations how he was converted," Gipsy Smith suggested in one of his sermons.

Modest man Matthew must have been, for in the pages of his Gospel of Christ one does not see much of the man, Matthew. Whereas the rest of the evangelists are careful to mention the honor of *Matthew's* apostleship, but speak of his former dishonest and disgraceful course of life under the name *Levi,* Matthew himself sets it all down under his proper and common name, Matthew.

Matthew was a man of means before his conversion to Christ, but that plentitude was earned by Matthew in his position of publican or tax collector. Tax collector! Such a person and such a position were hated with a hot heart by every Jew. The Jew had nothing but disdain and disgust, despising such men so despicably that when they desired to reject or insult any individual, they would hurl this stinging, slurring indictment, "Let him be to thee as a heathen and as a publican."

But the deepest demonstration of Hebrew hatred of publicans went farther than insulting epithets. Jews considered and called publicans traitors to the Hebrew cause and faith, counted publican money tainted and unacceptable in the synagogue, and refused to consider any tax collector's testimony in their courts.

It would be easy to understand the Hebrews' hatred of publicans, for they were Jews who served the Roman government which occupied Israel. The Roman officials levied a tax and the publicans collected the tax, adding a percentage for their own personal profit. Such a system lent itself to unscrupulous, outrageous extortion by many publicans. Also, the publican could enforce his exorbitant fee by employing the Roman soldiers to exact the tax by force—even to imprisoning the individual, if necessary.

Matthew, a Jew, was one of those vilified Roman tax officials, very likely collecting taxes from the fishermen and from the merchants traveling the road through Capernaum.

In light of his contemptible and corrupted position, it is easy to see why Matthew's conversion to Christ would be a crisis experience in his life. To accept this call of Christ to salvation and service for Him would pose many problems to Matthew. The price tag was costly! As one well wrote of this experience:

> He was not ignorant that he must exchange wealth for poverty, a custom house for a prison, and rich and powerful masters for a naked and despised Savior. But he overlooked all those considerations, left all his interests and relations to become our Lord's disciple and to embrace a more spiritual life.

The Scriptures strongly suggest it was an immediate sellout to the Savior on Matthew's part. There were no questions, no hesitation, no reservations. All his hope of riches, position, power; all his house; all his business; all his record books; all his friends; all his family—he left all to follow Jesus!

Evidently the first evangelism of that newfound follower and his newfound faith was a farewell feast that Matthew made for his friends. He wanted them to meet and be ministered unto by his new Master. Matthew's friends, you may be sure, were not marked by spirituality and piety. They were publicans and politicians, gold-greedy,

117

power-grasping men, worldly, often wanton in their wickedness, sinners of every stripe.

No account is given of any converts to Christ, or what the reaction or response of those guests was. The festive meal did provoke the Pharisees to question, "Why eateth your master with publicans and sinners?" Such "legalists never understand the grace of God to the undeserving and the utterly lost."

Doubtlessly, Matthew's chief contribution to Christianity was his Gospel, which was "definitely the connecting link between the prophets of old and the new dispensation of grace." It was in a special sense the Jewish Gospel, with sixty Old Testament references, many allusions to the Old Bible, and more direct quotations from the Old Testament than Mark and Luke combined. A. T. Robertson, New Testament expert, says: "The book is probably the most useful one ever written; it comes first in the New Testament collection, and has done more than any other to create the impression of Jesus that the world has obtained."[1]

How many multiplied Jews have claimed Christ as their Messiah and Redeemer because of Matthew's great Messianic writings under the Holy Spirit only Heaven's records will reveal. Great hosts of Gentiles as well have found soul rest in the Savior from such earnest entreaties as Matthew 11:28-30, among others. And multiplied masses of missionaries have been motivated to seek lost souls across the street and across the seas under Christ's clarion call and commission to evangelize, recorded in Matthew 28:18-20.

The Scriptures cite nothing of Matthew's ministry or of his death after the record of the resurrection of Christ. Tradition tells us that Matthew preached in Judaea then Ethiopia, where he was supposedly martyred. But whether in life or death, preaching, praying, personal work or penning gospel good news, one is safe in suggesting about Matthew: he forsook all to follow Christ!

NOTE:

1. J. Sidlow Baxter, *Explore the Book,* 6 vols. (Grand Rapids: Zondervan Publishing House, 1973), 5:160.

Paul

Evangelism's Prince

Beyond anyone's denial or dispute are these words rightly written about the apostle Paul:

> The Apostle Paul is by universal consent recognized as the finest product of the Gospel and the greatest man made by the creative and re-creative power of God. . . . His influence in the world today after twenty centuries is next to Christ's. He is God's most powerful advocate and exponent. He ranks first in the world's long list of evangelists.[1]

The Scripture story of Paul's life reads more like fantastic fiction than the Spirit-of-God inspired fact that it is. It is doubtful if any mortal man lived a life that was more eventful, more essential in its purpose, or more eternal in its result than this chiefest of sinners who became the choicest of soul-winners, the peer of preachers and the prince of evangelists.

"Chief of sinners." That was Paul's own appraisal of himself before his conversion to Christ. That was not a false-humility evaluation, for Paul cataloged his crimes against Christ, Christians and the church before his salvation thusly: "murderer," "persecutor," "blasphemer" and "injurious." The Scriptures further charge him with these acts of atrocity: "Made havock of the church, entering into every house, and haling men and women committed them to prison," "breathing out threatenings and slaughter against the disciples of the Lord."

But Paul (or Saul) got saved! On the Damascus Road—with letters of authority to find Christians, bind them and bring them to Jerusalem and judgment—Saul was stricken down, smitten in his sins and saved! This was doubtlessly the climax of all conversions to Christ. That day God emptied His arsenal of soul-winning artillery to apprehend this arch-criminal against Christ.

Paul's conversion was cataclysmic! One minute he was the chiefest of sinners, the next moment he was a child of God. One minute he was an avowed enemy of Christ, the next moment he was an aggressive evangelist of the faith he had so desperately, so dedicatedly, so diabolically tried to destroy! At once Paul became the ablest, best, choicest evangelist God ever called into that worthy work. There are at least three reasons why.

First, Paul had a vision of the living, lifted-up, loving Lord Jesus! That day he became Christ's bond slave, ready to be anything, ready to obey everything, ready to go everywhere at Christ's slightest will or wish (Rom. 1:14-16). Second, Paul had a vision of a lost world depraved in sin, doomed to death and to be damned in Hell. That day Paul sold out to soul winning: perennial, persistent, passionate soul winning. He was ever after impelled, compelled, propelled by "the love of Christ [which] constraineth us; because we thus judge, that if one died for all, then were all dead" (2 Cor. 5:14). Third, Paul had a vision of eternity. From that day on, Paul's life, labors, brain, brawn, aye, his best, were invested not for time, but for the "eternal weight of glory" (2 Cor. 4:17).

These transforming visions transported Paul in ever-widening spheres of service for Christ: Jerusalem, Antioch, Galatia, Macedonia, Rome, the world! As succinctly stated by another, "Paul's zeal to evangelize transcended all territorial, racial, national and political limitations."

Which statement causes me to consider Paul's methods in

evangelism. "I am made all things to all men, that I might by all means save some," penned Paul in 1 Corinthians 9:22. Believe it, Paul utilized any and every method that was worthy, workable and—it must be added—scriptural! The Pauline philosophy gives no allowance nor alibi for anyone practicing or participating in the "easy-come" ecumenical evangelism which is becoming more and more a curse to our churches and converts to Christ today!

Paul practiced personal evangelism—the man-to-man method of soul winning. He sought to win governors, kings, a demon-possessed girl, sailors, a runaway slave, soldiers, rulers of the synagogues. Paul preached! Any place he found people became a pulpit to proclaim Christ, whether it be a synagogue, in the streets, on board a ship, in schoolhouses, in prisons, before mobs, at Mars Hill.

And Paul practiced evangelism in every way as well as everywhere! In writings, in miracles, in teaching, in visitation, in making tents, in prayer—anywhere and everywhere—Paul was an all-out, always-at-it evangelist. No wonder at the end of his three-year ministry at Ephesus, he could triumphantly testify: "Wherefore I take you to record this day, that I am pure from the blood of all men" (Acts 20:26).

But Paul's method of evangelism included more than these elements. He perpetuated the results of his ministry. Roland Leavell has wisely observed:

> This foremost evangelist set the standard for evangelism for all succeeding generations by not stopping when the personal application of the gospel had won men to discipleship in Christ. He organized his converts into churches. He visited and revisited the converts, directed the ordination of ministers and deacons, admonished his followers in doctrine and morals. He personally trained young ministers to take up the torch of evangelism when it should fall from his failing hand.[2]

And Dr. Leavell correctly concluded: "The methods and the message of Paul must be more and more the methods and the message of the twentieth century apostles if Christian evangelists are to win people in great numbers to Jesus Christ."[3]

Amen! May the mantle of Paul—the man, his motivation, his message, his methods, yea, his Master—fall upon us today, I pray!

NOTES:

1. Scarborough, *With Christ After the Lost*, p. 67.
2. Roland Q. Leavell, *Evangelism: Christ's Imperative Commission* (Nashville: Broadman Press, 1951), p. 40. Used by permission.
3. Ibid., p. 41.

Peter

Pentecost's Preacher

Although my title is "Peter—Pentecost's Preacher," another word vies and cries for attention. That word is *paradoxical;* and, you believe it, Peter was paradox personified. Lee R. Scarborough pointedly penned of Peter:

> He was simple yet complex in his makeup. No one knew when he would break out in a new place. He would cower before a Jewish lass in his denial of Christ, and yet would face without a tremor an angry mob of ecclesiastics when his soul was set in the power of the Holy Spirit. He would face an infuriated gang of crucifiers with a sword at one moment and a little later play the coward when facing his duty to the deserted Savior.[1]

Yet despite his frailties and failures, Peter shared with the Savior a momentous and mighty ministry that no other evangelist can ever hope to experience. Even his conversion and call to preach were unique occasions such as only a favored few have ever known. First, Peter was a personal convert of Christ Himself. Brought by his brother Andrew to meet the Messiah, Peter—a young, married, arrogant, bragging, cursing, swaggering fisherman—was convicted of his sins, committed his soul to the Savior, and was converted the first time he met the Master. That day Peter became a disciple of Christ.

A few short months later, at a seashore, Peter, who "had been wont to make his own plans, follow his own chart, take his own course, and master his own craft," sat under the ministry of his Savior again. This time Christ called Peter to preach, to "become a fisher of men," to "launch out into the deep, and let down [his] nets for a draught." At first there was question, hesitation, contradiction on the part of Peter, but consummately conquered by that call, constrained to do the will of his Lord, Peter honestly and wholly turned over the entire command of his life to Christ and soul winning as he sobbed out, "nevertheless at thy word I will. . . ." That day Simon Peter became an evangelist!

It was not easy. There were lessons to learn. Although likable, loving by nature, a born leader in ability, Peter was, at the same time, uncouth, unlettered, unpredictable and untried. But under the tireless, transforming tutelage of the Lord, Peter was slowly but surely prepared to be worthy and worthwhile in the high and holy ministry to which Christ called him: an apostle, a penman of two New Testament epistles and a soul-winning preacher and evangelist!

May I remind you—it took messages, mighty messages; it took penetrating parables; it took powerful pleadings and the personal prayers of Christ; and it took multiplied mighty miracles by the Lord: the raising of Lazarus from the dead, Christ's walking on the water, the finding of the fish with the tax money in its mouth, the curse on the fig tree, the feeding of the multitudes, the transfiguration, yea, the resurrection and ascension of the Lord Jesus; it took a broken heart of repentance by Peter and the personal, precious restoration of that defecting and denying disciple by the living Lord; and it took a ten-day prayer meeting—all combined in the crucible of Calvary to make Simon Peter a soul-winning, worthy evangelist.

But, bless the Lord, Peter made one! Yes, he made one of God's greatest evangelists! "One of God's greatest" is not just a superlative and superfluous statement, for Simon Peter was the preacher at two soul-winning services that no evangelist can ever possibly experience again.

It was Evangelist Peter who preached the first sermon ever given to a Gentile congregation (Cornelius and his household, Acts 10), thus becoming the human instrument under God that ushered in the Gentile dispensation of worldwide, whosoever-will evangelism.

But it was as Pentecost's proclaimer that Peter became a peer among preachers. On the Day of Pentecost Peter preached the "first sermon in the world under the vice-regency of the Holy Spirit."[2] It was a sermon of 531 words—words so piercing, so pungent under Holy Spirit empowering that the bold, blatant, blasphemous men who had crucified Christ became so convicted of their cardinal crime they interrupted the sermon and cried out in consummate contrition," What shall we do?" And at the evangelist's earnest exhortation, "Repent, and be baptized every one of you in the name of Jesus Christ for the remission of sins, and ye shall receive the gift of the Holy Ghost" (Acts 2:38), about 3,000 sinners were saved.

May I suggest another supernal result of that sermon by Simon Peter? That little crowd of 120 courageous Christians who stood with Peter that day against all the military might and political power of the Roman empire, and against all the ecclesiastical power and prestige of the Sanhedrin and a Jewish nation which had already crucified Christ and was diligently dedicated to destroying His every disciple, realized another mighty miracle. That heroic handful was forged by the baptizing fire of the Holy Spirit into a church: a militant, evangelistic church—a church that, by the grace of God, has not only endured the onslaughts of Satanic opposition for nineteen centuries, but has also, by the power of God, evangelized multiplied millions of sinners, literally saving these souls from a devil's infernal, eternal Hell to the Savior's heavenly home and eternal hope!

May the stirring, shining example of that first-century evangelist and his bold and brave band challenge our churches in this twentieth century to renew, yea, redouble our evangelism, storming the citadels of sin: calling, teaching, preaching in the power of the same Holy Spirit and experiencing the same precious promise from the same Commander and Christ: "the gates of hell shall not prevail against [you]" (Matt. 16:18).

NOTES:

1. Scarborough, *With Christ After the Lost,* p. 63.
2. Ibid., p. 64.

Philip

Layman Evangelist

Philip was probably the first of a long line of those soul-winning worthies whom we call today by the term "laymen evangelists"; men who make their livelihood in the secular world but give largely of their time and talents to proclaiming the gospel good news. Philip was not an apostle, but was one of the original seven men the church at Jerusalem ordained to be deacons. From the qualifications of deacons as set forth in Acts 6:3, Philip would have had to be a man of "honest report, full of the Holy Ghost and wisdom."

Philip was also a man endued with the evangelistic gift, because the Scriptures relate of his successes in a great revival effort in Samaria:

> And the people with one accord gave heed unto those things which Philip spake, hearing and seeing the miracles which he did. For unclean spirits, crying with loud voice, came out of many that were possessed with them: and many taken with palsies, and that were lame, were healed. And there was great joy in that city. . . . But when they believed Philip preaching the things concerning the kingdom of God, and the name of Jesus Christ, they were baptized, both men and women (Acts 8:6-8, 12).

No ear-tickling, easy-come, easy-go evangelist was lay-preacher Philip! With what power, passion and purpose Philip must have preached the Person of Christ! Age old Samaritan-Jewish prejudices were healed, demon-possessed sinners were delivered, revival fires were ignited, believers were baptized, the city rejoiced, and Christ was glorified! May Philip's breed and brand of preaching permeate our churches, our classrooms and our city streets is my prayer!

But Philip was more than a man mighty in public ministry. He is also pictured in the Bible as a paramount example of personal evangelism. There is no more thrilling story in the Scriptures than Acts 8:26-39, where we read of Philip's masterful ministry in pointing the politically important Ethiopian sinner to a saving knowledge of the Lord Jesus Christ. Philip's sensitivity to the Holy Spirit and his submissiveness to the will of God are never better seen than when he selflessly left the popularity, the pull and the pleasures of the "big" and "important" revival meeting in Samaria to travel the many wearying and seeming wasted miles to a lonely, desert highway near Gaza. But Philip went *where* he was told, *when* he was told, without asking *why*.

There Philip met a hungry-hearted, heavy-hearted Ethiopian eunuch, treasurer of his land, returning home from Jerusalem without help or hope for his sinful and sorrowful soul. Philip joined himself to the sinner and his chariot, realized the eunuch could not understand the Scripture he was reading (Isaiah 53), and beginning at that passage presented Christ to the salvation-seeking sinner.

The Scriptures record of that holy hour that the sinner believed the Bible message, received the Lord Jesus as Savior, obeyed the Lord in believer's baptism, and went the rest of his way home rejoicing! History's chronicles record that this one convert carried the gospel back to his country, resulting in converts to Christ and churches organized to continue the evangelism launched by a layman preacher, a deacon who dared to do his duty!

At least two lucid lessons should be learned from the life of Philip, the evangelist. I share with you some sentences by Lee Scarborough as penned in his excellent book *Endued To Win*. May they speak to our hearts and to our help:

First: GOD ENDORSES THE LAYMAN EVANGELIST. Here is a scriptural illustration of the Divine approval upon a deacon holding evangelistic meetings, and doing roadside evangelism. We need more such evangelists. The coming of Christ's kingdom would be greatly hastened if the churches would send out more of their strong laymen one by one, their young people in groups to nearby communities, to hold soul-winning campaigns.

Second: THE DUTY OF PASTORS TO DEACONS. It is evident that Pastor James and the apostles did much for these deacons in training them in the Scriptures and in the art of soul winning; and here is a worthy New Testament example set for the pastors of all generations. The pastor should train his deacons in winning souls and backing the church in all its spiritual enterprises. The deacons are to do more than take care of the temporalities of the church. . . . They are to cooperate with the pastor in the spiritualities of the church. Blessed is the pastor who knows how and will take time and exercise patience in carefully training his board of deacons in the spiritual work of Christ's kingdom.[1]

NOTE:

1. Scarborough, *Endued To Win,* p. 256.

Priscilla and Aquila

Team Evangelism

One of the constantly amazing discoveries about new methods of evangelism and Christian education in our twentieth century is their *antiquity* rather than their *originality!* I refer to two of our "modern" concepts: one known in Sunday school ministry as "team teaching," and also the innovation in evangelism of "advance evangelists" who precede the evangelist—organizing, training workers, promoting and finalizing the program so everything is ready for the entrance of the evangelist and his party to reap the harvest.

May I introduce you to a couple who practiced these same ministries nineteen centuries ago: Priscilla and Aquila! Our first glimpse of them in the gospel story is in Acts 18:1-3. In this account of Paul's second missionary journey, he meets this married couple in Corinth. Corinth was a seat of government, a center of trade and transportation, a most logical place to commence a ministry that could fan out to every corner of the world. Aye, but it was also a sin city, a saturnalia of some of the vilest vices known in human history. There was situated the famed temple dedicated to Aphrodite, or Venus, called the temple of the thousand vestal virgins, but in fact the temple of libertine lust—the religion of sex worship. Correspondingly, Corinth was corrupted with drink, drunkenness, debauchery; in all actuality, Corinth was a devil's den. Its profligacy was proverbial in that ancient world. Paul had gone there under divine directive to evangelize it and organize a church to the glory of Christ.

One of his early contacts was with Priscilla and Aquila. They, with thousands of other Jews, had been evicted from Rome under the edict of Claudius. As one worthy wrote: "Surely there is a Providence of contact!" Aquila and his wife might have gone several directions when they fled Rome—for instance to Pontus, place of his birth, or any of the many great cities—but the two converged on Corinth. Some short time later Paul came to the same city and he "found Aquila, perhaps in a Jewish Guild of Trades, and was at once attracted to him because he was a Jew, a Christian and a tentmaker."

Aquila was a weaver of goat's hair tent cloth, called "cilicium" (or haircloth from Cilicia). This weaving was done on long looms, fifty feet or more in length. Paul abode in the couple's home and worked at the same trade. On the Sabbath he reasoned with the Jews in the synagogue, converting some from Judaism, along with some Gentiles. He organized that embryo group into the church of Corinth. Whether Aquila and Priscilla were Christians before Paul met them in Corinth is debatable. Scripture says nothing of their conversion. It is for sure if they were not already saved before leaving Rome, they became converts to Christ under Paul's personal witness, preaching and persuading ministry in Corinth.

Permit a profile of Priscilla. Evidently she was a Roman lady of rank. In the six Scripture citations of the two, Priscilla's name is given first in four of the accounts. This was not a courtesy extended because of her sex, but rather an honor attributed her because of her social standing, as well as a reference to her evidently more dominant personality and importance.

Priscilla and Aquila not only housed Paul for eighteen months; they also opened their home to become a churchhouse for gospel meetings and worship of God. This had to be one of their first and finest contributions to the cause of evangelism in Europe.

It was at Ephesus that this Christ-honoring couple performed another service that thrust evangelism for Christ further into that western world. I refer to that beautiful and blessed Biblical account of Priscilla and Aquila taking in tow the youthful evangelist, Apollos, and tutoring him in "the way of God more perfectly." Briefly summarized, Apollos, an Alexandrian Jew, a mighty intellect in the Scriptures and an eloquent evangelist, but limited in his message and ministry, "knowing only the baptism of John," came to Ephesus. He preached powerfully, persuasively and passionately his message which embraced only the truths of the gospel known at John the Baptist's death: the person, deity and miracles of Christ and the necessity of repentance for sins and baptism in His name. It has to be one of Christian history's sweet and sacred stories: Aquila and Priscilla took the evangelist into their hearts and into their home. Instead of *upbraiding* him they *upgraded* him, instructing him more fully in the great areas of Christ's substitutionary death, His bodily resurrection and ascension, the Holy Spirit's coming, baptizing, filling, along with other vital Biblical truths.

To the praise of Apollos, that gifted, anointed youth humbled himself, listened and learned from his elders, two who were far less eloquent, far less endowed with evangelism's gifts. And to the praise of Priscilla and Aquila, they accepted Apollos for what he was, instructed him in what he should know and be, and then encouraged him and opened to him the potentiality of his great ministry by commending him to others.

Aquila and Priscilla were team teachers on the highest, holiest plane. They set the pattern for the husband and wife teams today who minister in our Sunday schools, children's churches and bus ministries—teaching, training and thrusting out into Christian service a host of youth *reached* for the Savior, *saved* by the Savior and *dedicated* to serve the Savior! Workers like an Aquila and Priscilla will see themselves multiplied in some like Apollos who, in his day, "blazed like a comet of ecclesiastical heavens at Ephesus and Corinth struck down opposition and unbelief with the onslaught of his fervid and logical eloquence."

But doubtlessly Priscilla and Aquila's greatest contribution to evangelism's spearheading thrust through the western world was in their ministry as "advance evangelists" for the apostle Paul. William Sanford LaSor spoke of this evangelism that ever enlarged the circle of Christianity:

Paul had his heart set on going to Ephesus. He had seen it as the strategic

130

place to locate the Gospel (but he had been prevented from going there by the Spirit's direction—Acts 16:6). It became clear to him that Ephesus had to precede Rome in his itinerary. . . . It was his custom to go to Jerusalem as often as possible to participate in the religious festivals . . . so he planned to make his pilgrimage from Corinth, before taking up the work in Ephesus. But meanwhile he would get the work started there; and this he did by the simple expedient of taking Priscilla and Aquila to Ephesus and leaving them there while he went to Jerusalem (Acts 18:14-19).[1]

Aquila and Priscilla had all the spiritual resources necessary for such a ministry. Paul had learned of their zeal, devotion, knowledge of the Scriptures and the basics of the Christian faith, their compassion and hospitality in his nearly two-year residence with them in Corinth. And as LaSor added:

They could settle down in Ephesus in their trade, lay the groundwork for Paul, until he could get to Ephesus (c.f. Acts 18:21). I can see no other reason for rooting them up from their important work in Corinth.

Priscilla and Aquila were in Ephesus during all of Paul's extended stay in that city—the church met in their home—then suddenly a few months later Priscilla and Aquila were in Rome when Paul wrote the Epistle to the Romans toward the end of his third missionary journey. Why? I can think of only one satisfactory reason—Paul was using the same strategy for Rome he had used for Ephesus. He was sending Priscilla and Aquila on ahead in order that the groundwork would be laid for his arrival. What he did not know at the time was that a two year delay would be occasioned by his imprisonment in Caesarea.[2]

It is scripturally evident that the two succeeded in their work at Rome for Paul and the Lord. Paul, writing to those Roman Christians, praised this couple with whom he had resided, eaten, prayed, worked and worshiped in other cities: "Greet Priscilla and Aquila my helpers in Christ Jesus: Who have for my life laid down their own necks [where, when and how, Scripture does not state]: unto whom not only I give thanks, but also all the churches of the Gentiles. Likewise greet the church that is in their house" (Rom. 16:3-5). Aye, Priscilla and Aquila were always, everywhere the faithful, fruitful couple for Christ!

Christian historians herald this heroic couple, and rightly so. Archbishop Evans expressed appreciation "on the profitable usefulness of Priscilla, especially in reference to female converts, and the training of deaconesses." McGiffert mentioned:

They furnish us the most beautiful example known in the Apostolic age of the power of God that could be exerted by a husband and wife working in unison for the advancement of the Gospel.

Their home was always open for the church to meet in their house.

They were always ready to go where God wanted them. They were ready to lose themselves in the footnotes of history. But their influence was clearly felt in the greatest cities of their day. Here is an example for any young couple to follow!

NOTES:

1. William S. LaSor, *Great Personalities of the New Testament: Their Lives and Times* (Westwood, NJ: Fleming H. Revell, 1961), p. 142.
2. Ibid., p. 143.

Samaritan Woman

Evangelism Reaching the Alienated

I was tempted to title this profile "A Study of E.R.A."—not to be construed as a study of the Equal Rights Amendment, an evangelism of which there are appeals aplenty in this decade. For my purposes E.R.A. spells out "Evangelism Reaching the Alienated," because that is the thrust of John 4.

The Bible is the greatest textbook on soul-winning evangelism (the whys, the wherefores and the hows). Doubtless the greatest chapter in that greatest chronicle on how to convert sinners to Christ is

John's Gospel, the fourth chapter. The ABC's, the 1,2,3s of personal evangelism fill the verses of that chapter. The motives, the message and the methods of successful soul winning are magnified by the master evangelist, the Lord Jesus Christ Himself. Any reader desirous of fruitful and effective personal evangelism will do well to read, reread, review, rehearse, practice and persist in Christ's example of evangelism recorded in John 4.

Consider Christ as seen in that text. Concern for a lost soul had driven Him into the alien land of the Samaritans, people half-breed Jew and Gentile, foreigners to the Jewish faith and fellowship, deniers and despisers of the true worship of Jehovah with their own temple and all its idolatrous and iniquitous trappings. So it is seen that Samaritans were outcasts to the orthodox Jews—racially, religiously, socially. But the Scriptures state of the Savior: "And he must needs go through Samaria." The reason is evident. Christ's purpose, passion of life was "to seek and to save that which was lost," and a woman would be at Jacob's well that day at the noon hour. The soul-hungry Savior must meet her.

The Scripture shows that Christ was weary and worn, hungry and thirsty. Lee Scarborough scripturally stated, "There was enough human in Him to tire; but, thank God, not enough to sin."[1] He had dispatched His disciples to Sychar, the nearby city, for food and refreshment for that noon-hour meal at the well mouth.

Momentarily the woman arrived alone. Bible paragraphs give a probing, penetrating picture of that woman at the well. In today's sin-soaked society that Samaritan woman would be a heroine, pictures headlining newspapers, interviews permeating television shows, life exposés glutting the magazines and periodicals. But in that day she was a looked-down-on, loathed and lonely harlot. Thus she would rather brave the burning, blistering noonday sun alone at the well to get her waterpot filled than to have to face the scorching, searing, sneering looks of the other women who came to the well at the cooler evening hour. Yes, see a sin-saddened, sin-sated soul, with a hungering, heavy heart. As one so well and wisely wrote, "There can be no sadder picture than the picture of fallen virtue. When sin puts the scarlet letter on the face of fair womanhood the picture is changed from the highest beauty and choicest personality to the vilest and most depraved."[2] Right! Witness this woeful woman: harlot, hopeless, possibly homeless, surely helpless, heartsore and hellbound!

The total conversation seen in the Scriptures between Christ and the woman is an epic in evangelism. Limited space necessitates only limited reference. Suffice it to say here, Christ converted her! That

134

conversion was *complete* conversion—she was saved all the way in, all the way out, all the way up, all the way down, all the way around, all the way through—six-dimensional salvation! That salvation saved her soul from Hell to Heaven, saved her life from a love for sin and Satan to a love for Christ and a life for His service and soul winning.

In my mind's eye many times I have tried to survey that scene as that newborn, blood-washed, salvation-assured, every-sin-cleansed convert thrillingly and thankfully ran back to Sychar as fast as her feet could fly to witness to the men she had sinned *with* and sinned *against*, "Come, see a man, which told me all things that ever I did: is not this the Christ?"

I confess that because of that statement and question I read and reread the whole account over and over again seeking to find where Christ indicted her of her every iniquity. And I found NOWHERE! It is as Spurgeon said:

> She was right. Were you ever out in a black and murky night when a single lightning flash has come? It has only smitten one oak in the field but in so doing has revealed all the landscape. It struck one object but all around you is light as day for a moment. So when the Lord Jesus revealed this woman's lustfulness, she saw clearly the whole of her life at a single view; and the Lord God indeed told her all things that she had ever done. Do you wonder that she said, "Is this not the Christ?"[3]

Her simple, single message caused a city to hear the gospel and resulted in a host believing on Christ to the converting of their souls also. A revival swept that ancient and alienated city because of a woman's word about her newfound Lover and Lord. I find myself wondering how many other converts to Christ can claim similar results because of a similar warning, warm witness to the old, unconverted crowd.

The chapter is abrim with thrilling and transcendent truths, but I cite only one suggested by Lee Scarborough:

> There is another message luminous here . . . and that is the need of wayside evangelism. There are women [and men] at many wellsides needing some messenger of the Messiah to open up the fountains of eternal life. My prayer is that [someone] will form in his or her heart the passion for wayside evangelism. We have changed the Gospel from its early method, I fear. We have limited its proclamation to the four walls of synagogues and churches. We should carry it out to the needs of men. . . . May the example of the Savior here as well as His Samaritan convert cause you and me not to neglect the passers-by, the strangers we meet, the needy, the fallen, the suffering everywhere.[4]

NOTES:

1. Scarborough, *How Jesus Won Men,* p. 73.
2. Ibid., p. 75.
3. Charles H. Spurgeon, *The Metropolitan Tabernacle Pulpit* (Pasadena, TX: Pilgrim Publications, 1973), vol. 28, p. 502.
4. Scarborough, *How Jesus Won Men,* p. 86.

Timothy

Teenage Preacher Boy

Although he was a lesser light since he ministered in the shadows of the illustrious apostle Paul, the man known only by the Bible title of Timothy was nevertheless one of the leading lights of evangelism in the first century.

Timothy was converted to Christ by Paul and was a close companion to the aging apostle in many of his ministries. He conducted campaigns in churches of Greece and Asia, preparing the way for the apostle Paul's coming ministry or following up his ministry in other instances. Truly Timothy was an evangelist and did the work of an evangelist in excellent degree.

Timothy was eminently equipped for his unique ministry of evangelism to both Jews and Greeks to whom he ministered. Born of a Gentile father and a Jewish mother, "his mixed descent formed a link between Jews and Gentiles," giving him a vital rapport with both peoples.

Timothy's conversion occurred during the apostle Paul's first missionary ministry in the area known as Lycaonia in Asia Minor. Timothy had been thoroughly taught in the Old Testament Scriptures, although he had never been circumcised into the Jewish faith. However, that earnest, honest teaching of his mother, Eunice, and that of his grandmother, Lois, coupled with their unfeigned faith, had prepared the soul of teenager Timothy to the place that when the peerless Paul preached the great good news of the gospel of the crucified, buried and resurrected Jesus Christ, pointing out that Christ was the fulfillment of the Old Testament prophecies, the young Timothy took Christ as his Messiah and Lord! How many other conversions Paul may have experienced in his evangelism through Lycaonia we know not, but it is safe to say that Timothy was born into the faith, a child of God who one day would also become the one whom Paul would own "as a son with the father, he hath served with me in the gospel."

It was some six or seven years later that this relationship was established. Paul returned to Lystra and, when he was getting an accounting of the converts of his prior ministry there, must have been most gratified to learn that Timothy had been well trained and was well reported of the brethren. Perceiving that Timothy had the marks, the makings and the message as a preacher of the gospel, Paul set apart the probably twenty-year-old youth for the ministry by the laying on of hands.

When Paul left Lystra, he took Timothy with him, a trip that was to commence a ministry for Christ that would eventuate in evangelism across Greece, Asia, and possibly into Rome, and would end as tradition tells in martyrdom after imprisonment. Specific areas of ministry of Timothy are seen in the Scriptures as Troas; Berea; Athens, the philosophical city; Thessalonica; Ephesus, the oriental city; Galatia; Antioch, the commercial city; Phrygia; Jerusalem; Macedonia; Philippi, the colonial city; Corinth, the maritime city; and Rome, the imperial city.

Nothing, or next to nothing, is known of Timothy's preaching or of his results. We have no recorded messages or even excerpts of his messages. But it is not possible that Paul would have trusted Timothy to such strategic situations and important centers and cities if Timothy had not had the ministry, methods, message and motives for such essential evangelism. Possibly his ministry at Ephesus, with all its perils and perplexities, where he was sent by Paul, that he might "charge some that they teach no other doctrine," gives us some hint as to the heart, spirit, and type of ministry Timothy had and to the supreme confidence Paul placed in him.

That confidence was centered in a youth whose ministry and makeup had early weaknesses. E. A. Litton wrote:

> The circumstances of his education seem to have imparted a feminine tenderness to his character, coupled with a degree of timidity which needed the support of apostolic authority (1 Corinthians 16:10, 11) and sometimes apostolic admonitions (1 Timothy 4:12). This perhaps rose partly from a weakly constitution (1 Timothy 5:23). Yet the defect must have been faithfully striven against, for none of the apostolic delegates were more incessantly engaged in active service or more important missions.

That Timothy had a special place in the heart of the aged apostle is seen in this pithy, pathos-filled line from Paul's last letter: "To Timothy, my dearly beloved son: . . . without ceasing I have remembrance of thee in my prayers night and day; greatly desiring to see thee, being mindful of thy tears, that I may be filled with joy" (2 Tim. 1:2-4).

Jesus Christ

Soul-Winner Supreme

Evangelism is seen at once to be the one essential element in the earthly ministry of our Lord. His birth, His baptism, His heart's burden, His life's blood, His very breath; yea, His entire being were all centered in the supreme task of evangelism—soul-winning evangelism!

He was born against the backdrop of evangelism. The night of His birth brought angels their one and only opportunity to engage in evangelism; and from the glory-filled skies they proclaimed to a fallen race of dying men, "For unto you is born this day in the city of David a Saviour, which is Christ the Lord" (Luke 2:11). And that same night, soul-thrilled shepherds who had heard the angelic message and had found and had seen their Savior, became earnest evangelists, "making known abroad" what their ears had heard, what their eyes had seen, and what their hearts had felt!

When Jesus began His public ministry, it was in the climate of evangelism, for He chose to be introduced by an evangelist, John the Baptist. Lee Scarborough pointedly penned of this incident:

> His forerunner, John the Baptist, was an evangelist, preeminently a soul winner. He was not a teacher. He was not a healer of the bodies of men. He seemed to have one objective and that was the salvation of the souls of men from sin. And it was in this atmosphere, the soul-winning atmosphere in which he introduced Jesus. John was one of God's topmost evangelists and stands through the centuries as the first in his field. It is significant and indicative of the whole ministry of Christ that He should be thus introduced by a soul-winning evangelist![1]

Rightly so! For evangelism was the energizing thrust of Jesus' ministry. Soul-winning evangelism was the impelling power that caused Christ to come from Heaven. R. G. Lee, in lucid lines, tells us truly:

> From the heights of deity to the depths of humanity; from the glory place to the gory place, Jesus came to die a criminal's death. Seeking the lost—soul saving—is the only business big enough to bring Jesus out of the ivory palaces into this world of woe; leaving the honors of Heaven for the horrors of the cross, giving up the adorations of Heaven for the abominations of the earth, relinquishing the joy of Heaven for the jeers of wicked men.[2]

These are not just pretty phrases, for Christ appraised the purpose of His coming to earth in similar speech that spelled out evangelism: "For the Son of man is come to seek and to save that which was lost" (Luke 19:10). But you believe this: If evangelism was the impelling power that caused Christ to come to earth, it was also the propelling, compelling passion that constrained Him to tirelessly tramp up and down the streets and lanes of the city, fan out farther into the highways and hedges of the countryside, and then go on in ceaseless calling from city to city, teaching, preaching, healing, seeking, saving the lost (Matt. 9:35; Mark 1:32-39).

Nothing could deter Christ from evangelism, not even the acclaim of the thronging, teeming crowds who came to see and hear Him. He must press on: "Let us go into the next towns, that I may preach there also: for therefore came I forth" (Mark 1:38). Nothing could

141

discourage Him in evangelism—not even the failures of the many half-hearted followers who would faint under privations or persecutions by priests and people. Nothing could defeat Christ in evangelism. His face was set as a flint with resolute purpose to win lost souls: a Philip, a Simon Peter, a Matthew, a Nicodemus, a scarlet Samaritan harlot, a Zacchaeus, a Bartimaeus, a Gadarene maniac. The sinner may be under a tree, up a tree, in the marketplace, at the seashore, in the home, at a well, on a dusty highway, or in a cemetery; but Jesus was dedicated to seeking sinners whoever and wherever they might be!

John R. Rice warmingly wrote of Christ:

> Lost sinners were on the mind and heart of the Savior all the time. If a Jewish woman lost one of the string of dowry coins, Jesus thought of a lost soul. If a shepherd found one of his sheep missing, Jesus thought of a poor sinner away from God. If a boy was a wastrel and prodigal, Jesus saw him typical of every lost soul away from the Father's house. When He saw the sower sowing the seed, He thought of a soul winner. When He saw the fish in the net, He thought of catching men.

But if evangelism was the purpose, the practice—yea, the passion of Christ's life—believe it when I say that His life's blood was poured out in death for evangelism. He came to die for souls. As He Himself said, "The Son of man came not to be ministered unto, but to minister, and to give his life a ransom for many" (Matt. 20:28). One worthy wrote, "Christ would even stop dying to get a sinner saved!" And that is exactly what He did, as recorded in Luke 23:32-46. In His last living moments, this dying Sacrifice for sinners saw the hopeless condition of a convicted criminal on another cross, heard his penitent plea for mercy and pardoned his sins, promising him Heaven. That criminal on a cross was Christ's last personal hand-picked convert. At what awful cost He "snatched him as a brand from the burning fires of Hell."

Which thought prompts me to present this tremendous truth: This crucified Christ—buried, resurrected from the dead, ascended on high to Heaven; one soon, sure day to return, to receive Christians to Himself, to reward them for their labors, and to rule and reign over the world forever—is still calling, still commissioning His own to FOLLOW HIM in evangelism. It is the same call that inspired Andrew—a babe in his newfound faith—to be baptized in the stream of soul-winning evangelism and go, find, witness to and win his brother, Simon Peter, who would win others, who in turn would warn and win others in a never-ending, ever-widening sphere of soul-winning activity.

Suffice it to say, no one can—and no one ever will—write the biography of Christ, for "He ever liveth." And in the truest sense, no one will ever be able to write a biography of one of His soul-winning disciples, for "they that turn many to righteousness [shall shine] as the stars for ever and ever" (Dan. 12:3). Who will follow in His train?

NOTES:

1. Scarborough, *How Jesus Won Men,* p. 27.
2. R. G. Lee, *Bought by the Blood* (Grand Rapids: Zondervan Publishing House, 1957), p. 107.

DE D